WHAT MOMMY NEVER TOLD YOU

A Woman's Guide to the Next Phase of Life

By Ericka Pittman

This book is dedicated to the most amazing woman I have ever known. My mother, Pamela Pittman has been intentional, dedicated and on purpose about her guidance from the moment I was born. She made sure I knew I was loved and had the right to think for myself. She made sure I knew I was gifted and circumstances did not define me. I had the power to define myself.

Her unwavering commitment to rearing me has brought me 90% of the way and it is her love, honesty, and support that continues to push me over the balance.

Thank you Mommy for telling me what you could and for nurturing and pushing me along my journey to discover the rest on my own.

If I can become half the woman you have been I would step back and say "Job Well Done".

I love you to the moon and back again.

ACKNOWLEDGEMENTS

There are dozens of women that have made an imprint on my development, countless mother figures, friends, colleagues, and archetypes that I've modeled behavior against over the years. I thank you all equally, fully, and sincerely for every ounce of love, support, and example that you have poured into me.

I would like to make a special acknowledgment of my Aunt Terry for ALWAYS making me her priority, my Sister Tanya for loving me fiercely and unconditionally, my brother Shaun for being my companion, friend, and purpose, my amazing "Besties" for accepting all of my nuanced and often complex layers and loving every part of me, my godchildren Aaryn, Jaeden, Jarrett, Justin, Bailey, and Austin for bringing me so much pure joy, my good friends old and new and most importantly my sweet sweet Nana, Pearl V. Pittman, who has always been my "Best Judy" and continues on inspiring me to be my greatest self.

This book was born out of the love and support of some particularly amazing women who encouraged, inspired, coached, scolded and "midwifed" me through the entire process. Tomeka, thank you for gently pushing me to start over and make it to the finish line. Thank you to my entire family for all of the help and guidance you have offered . I could go on and on highlighting all of the people (men and women) who have touched my life for the better but I will leave you with this...

I love you all with all of my heart and I'm so incredibly blessed and grateful to have you.

Thank You!
Xoxo

EP

TABLE OF CONTENTS

FOREWORD

Throughout my childhood, one of my mom's favorite and most often used personal mantras was, "Show me the company you keep and I'll tell you the kind of person that you want to be." Elsa Miller's time-tested pearl of wisdom has never been more true than in the case of my friendship with Ericka Pittman.

From the moment Ericka and I met in New York City at the Vanguarde Media offices, I have admired her engaging personality, unquestionable intelligence, unshakeable value system, and relentless commitment to being her authentic self and living a joyful, balanced life. When Ericka walks into any room, she uplifts and envelops everyone within her reach in a genuine glow. As cliché as it may sound, Ericka is truly a beauty on the inside and out. Counting her amongst my closest friends is an honor… and responsibility.

You see, women like Ericka require more of friends and community than simply standing on the sidelines and cheering on her success in life. She has a loving — but firm — expectation of positivity, accountability, and constant betterment for all. Her commitment to empowering young women is irrefutable. Now, Ms. Pittman won't run your race for you… However, she will support you with honesty, kindness, humor, and compassion every step of the way.

She is determined to win but wants to do it alongside you. And she is truly happy to lend a hand to all those who are willing to do the work. What Mommy Never Told You is the outcome of that special energy.

Within these pages, Ericka is as forthcoming about her triumphs as she is about the challenges and losses along her journey. Her engaging anecdotes and lessons resonated with me, a fellow media professional who has spent many years as a journalist, editor and now, TV/film executive. But Ericka's realness will surely captivate readers of all walks of life as they gain insight into how to apply the knowledge from her experiences to their own circumstances. Through her "Pittman's Rules," she provides a clear and concise blueprint for anyone to use on their path to success.

Simply put, What Mommy Never Told You is the little bit of "Black Girl Magic" that will forever tip the scales in your favor. And I thank you, Ericka, for sprinkling a cup or two on all of us.

— Mitzi Miller

Chapter 1:
INTRODUCTION

This book is an ode to the incredible life that I have been given, to the beautiful spirit of my grandmother that is within me and to the purpose that I am here to fulfill. I want all young women to experience their greatest truth and realize their potential. The challenges and successes that I have experienced on this journey have taught me so many things — the good, the bad, and the ugly. I want to share that knowledge through the stories and lessons I have included in the coming chapters. This book is for every young woman who has a dream.

At the end of each chapter, I will recap everything that you need to take away from the lessons that I share. These will serve as quick references and a summary of the chapter to guide you, even if you are not able to read the entire book. Thank you for giving me the time and space in your life for me to share my experiences with you. Cheers to the best version of ourselves.

I am exactly where I need to be in life right now and so are you.

Whether you believe in God, the Source, the Universe or any other higher spiritual power, just trust the process of life even when you don't understand it. The natural order of things allows for infinite correlation, perfect orderliness, and evolution. In other words, everything is as it should be, and it will all work itself out in the end. Life is a journey, and everyone learns, grows and evolves on their own time. Each time that you evolve as a person or find yourself in a new situation, just know that you are exactly where you are supposed to be at that moment.

There are no mistakes in life. In fact, there is a hidden blessing and benefit in every circumstance you are dealt. If you can embrace that — you will start to manifest and live, despite fear, your greatest possibilities.

Life and business coach Marie Forleo summarized this perfectly when she said, "Show up in every single moment like you're meant to be there."

One of the most impactful moments in my life that awakened my faith and belief in the process was when my grandmother died. I got the call about my grandmother's passing when I was at the office having a conversation with Marilyn Van Alstyne, a vice president at Combs Enterprises at the time. In times of devastation and hardship, my default reaction is to be calm, unemotional and pragmatic. I received the news and immediately packed up my belongings and headed out the door without saying a word to Marilyn. She stopped me and said, "Where are you going?" I calmly answered, "My grandmother just passed away. I'm going to Brooklyn." And with that, I headed to my car and left. I didn't have a real emotion upon hearing the news because I knew she was gone. I was fortunate enough to have kissed her and said my goodbyes just a few short days before she passed.

In addition to being one of the most important role models in my life, my grandmother was my best friend, my confidante and my North Star. We had a special bond from the moment I was born. She was the person who always understood me, she had a sixth sense for what I needed and the things that weighed me down, even when I wasn't so sure myself. We had what I could only describe as a powerful karmic connection. We had this weird thing where I would simply think of her and she would call, or I would call her just as she was talking with someone else about me. We just got each other. My grandmother was my Meredith Grey and I was her Cristina Yang. She was my person and she will always be a part of my journey. I remember speaking at her burial service and assuring my family that she wasn't dead. I told them that she was a free spirit now and that she would always be with us. They all looked at me with concern, probably thinking, "Is she finally losing it?" I wasn't losing it. I just knew with certainty that her spirit would continue to stay and guide us. I feel her presence with me every day.

Even when I was an infant, my grandmother would write me postcards when she went on vacation. In my early years, she would read her messages to me because I couldn't read. She always talked to me like I was her best friend and I followed suit and did the same for her. When I got older and started working, my grandmother and I would reserve two weeks of our vacation time to spend with each other. Sometimes we flew over the ocean together to travel around the world, take road trips to different states together, and other times we would stay local and do things around the city. She created a special bond between us from the day I was born, and I will forever cherish it.

The day I lost my grandmother was the first time I truly understood the cycle of life and how short it can be. The saying "live for today" became central to my existence. I often find that it is out of devastation that evolution occurs. I was devastated in ways that I could not even put into words. It was like something died within me when she passed, but at the same time, it sparked a light inside of me that I didn't know existed. At that moment, the value I placed on my own life became real because I was living for her. It was the most difficult and inspiring experience I had gone through in my entire existence. This was the single moment that really tested how much I believed in the process of life and how willing I was to trust it. The day I lost my beloved grandmother was the day I began to truly live.

> " I often find that it is **out of devastation that evolution occurs.**

Prior to this day, I was living a great life — at least I had thought I was. I had what some would consider a successful and thriving career, an expanding personal brand, I was dining at some of the best restaurants around town, traveling to exotic locations, rubbing shoulders with the who's who of the world, and on and on I could go. It seemed as if I had it all — on paper at least. While I looked like I was winning at life, I wasn't living my fullest and greatest life. And it was the loss of my grandmother that kicked me in the gut. It made me realize that I needed to change, and I needed to do it fast.

When I reflected on the eclectic and vast sum of my grandmother's life, I realized that she lived the way she wanted to, even down to her very last breath. My grandmother even picked out her own funeral gown, a white-and-gold, full-length, sequined dress. That was the way she lived — full, out loud, self-expressed, boisterous and in love with life every single day.

My grandmother lived in full color. She vacationed the way she wanted, she laughed daily, and always had a circle of friends and family who loved her.

I still remember looking down at my grandmother's casket as I stood at the podium at her funeral, giving her eulogy. She lay in her beautiful gown looking content and satisfied. I didn't feel sad for her, I felt happy. I was at ease knowing that she had lived her life the way she wanted to, on her own terms. I fought to hold back my tears. Oddly enough they were not tears of sorrow, but instead tears of shame that I hadn't done the same with my own life in 36 years on this earth. At that moment I declared to all those in attendance at her funeral, and I had them repeat after me, "Live life out loud." In my declaration, I made a vow to my grandmother that I, too, would live life out loud, just like she'd done. This meant that I was going to stop playing small and start living the life of my dreams. I wasn't just going to make plans and not act on them, and I was going to start doing by living in the moment.

Even on her deathbed, my grandmother had a way of teaching and showing me the way. She was my first mentor and one of the most influential people in my life. It is because of this bond, that I always encourage women who come to me for mentorship to also look for mentorship from those who are already in their lives. Our earliest mentors come from within our own homes

> **"The day I lost my grandmother is the day I began to truly live.**

and families. While it's perfectly okay to admire the Oprah Winfreys and Michelle Obamas of the world, it is our earliest female influencers like our mothers, aunts, grandmothers, and sisters who know us best. These are the women we can look up to and model our own behaviors after because we see them up close, spend extensive time with them and absorb their lessons while sitting on their laps rather than those we admire from afar. Our loved ones shape who we become, and our character, in ways that only the greatest mentors can.

To this day, I use my grandmother's life as a yardstick. Now, years after her death, I continue to measure my actions and decisions based on the promise I made at her funeral. This hasn't been easy for me to do and if I'm being honest, I don't always fulfill on my promise to my grandmother. The truth is that I wrote this manuscript five years ago and had it shelved for years. I procrastinated and discouraged myself out of fear, out of lack of self-priority, and out of playing it small. I have not lived up to my vow to her over the past five years and for that, I am truly sorry.

You see, we are not always going to be perfect in life and we are not always going to live up to our word, but that's okay. The reality is that this book wasn't meant to happen five years ago. I hadn't lived enough. The journey to complete this book was supposed to happen just as it has happened. The divine order of things is powerful and undeniable. The key to a life well lived is to let it flow naturally. In doing so, you will learn to accept your past and allow your present to be aligned with what the Universe is trying to teach you.

On the last day of my grandmother's life, I understood for the first time how valuable our time on earth is. The true reality of each day hit me hard — every passing day was bringing me closer to the end of my own life. Yesterday already happened, tomorrow is still another day away, but today was and is the present — it is the most important time. "Today" is more precious than "someday." Not living in the moment perpetuates a vicious cycle of constant anticipation and delay. Stop waiting. Do it N.O.W. (No Other Way). The only way to action is to do it and you can't get it done until you start.

> "The key to a life well-lived is to **let it flow naturally.**

I lean on my loved ones, including my grandmother's spirit, to help me navigate the opportunities and challenges of life. I don't expect to go at it by myself and you shouldn't either. There is way too much to give and receive in this world to be alone. Human beings are meant to be in a community so don't be afraid to get the support you need from others. Asking for help is not a sign of weakness, but a source of power. You were blessed with many talents in this life, but that does not include every talent. There are people around you who are simply better at some things than you are, and asking for help from trusted sources can be extremely beneficial to your advancement. I ask that you allow me to be a part of your community and be open to the experiences and stories I am about to share with you. It may be unfamiliar, but I encourage you to hear me anyway and see yourself grow through our time together.

TRUST THE PROCESS

No matter how perfect my life may look now on the surface, it has been full of trials and tribulations and ugly moments. I have experienced loss, countless disappointments, betrayals, and heartbreaks just as much as any other human being. In all these moments though, what I have always been able to do is embody a spirit of resilience in knowing that there is a lesson in every experience. The faster I learned the lesson, the sooner God would push me into the next adventure. My "wins" are not the product of a sequence of well-orchestrated events or logical and calculated decisions. My life has been a constant roller coaster with highs, lows, deep dives, and smooth and steady moments. However, through it all, each moment has been perfect, even the lows and the deep dives. The best part of all my letdowns is that I am still standing and blessed with another chance to figure out this adventure called life. The biggest lesson I've come to learn is life does not happen to you, instead it happens for you.

One of these low moments, where I felt like my life took a deep dive for the worst, was when I was a teenager. I was just finishing high school and had the opportunity to go on a full academic scholarship to Spelman College in Atlanta, Georgia. My mother was vehemently against me going away to school, and she told me that if I went to Spelman, a poor choice in her mind because of its distance from our family home in New York, she would not support me at all in any way. I was told that if I left home and moved to Atlanta, then I would be on my own.

As a 17-year-old being told to support myself, I was scared. At that point, I was fully dependent on others. I had only known a life in which I was fully supported by my mother, so I had no idea what it would take to move out on my own. I hadn't had a job or made any money on my own, I hadn't lived on my own or paid any bills of my own. I had never been self-sufficient before and the idea of having to fend for myself without the support of my mother was something that terrified me. At that moment, I wanted to go to Spelman and experience life beyond Brooklyn, but fear stopped me. Fear made me small. And if we are being honest, fear of the unknown made my mother play small with my further education.

In her defense, my mother was just doing for me what she knew how to do. She let her own experiences determine what she thought was possible for me, and what she thought I could do on my own. As I reflect on that moment, I now know that she was just sharing what she knew at the time, with the tools she was equipped with. While my mother had a collegiate mandate in her house — it was college, or it was nothing — me going away and leaving home wasn't something she was ready to

> "Life does not happen to you, instead **it happens for you.**"

wrap her mind around. My mother worked diligently throughout her life to create a protected, safe home for me, one where she felt in control and could predict positive outcomes for me. The idea of me leaving so soon was too much for her at the time. I was far too young to understand the mental and emotional state my mother was experiencing. I just knew I had a chance to experience life and my mother was stifling my expansion. The experience made me feel trapped, confused, and resentful toward her.

I knew I had to go to college but was left with few options, so I applied to the City University of New York (CUNY). To buy myself time to figure things out, I went to a liberal arts school to get my associate's degree and I stayed with my family. My mother was ecstatic — I was going to college and staying at home. I had checked her boxes and that was enough for her. For me though, the entire experience made me feel limited. It made me realize that I needed to grow up, learn how to take care of myself, and become independent.

It took a few years for me to come to terms with the decision to go to college locally. I was secretly resentful and rebellious. At that point, I was pretty much over everything about Brooklyn. I hated the train, I loathed the projects, and I was done with looking over my shoulder walking through our neighborhood. I did not care for the doughboys on the corners trying their best to get my attention. I wanted more for my life, and I knew it was out there for me.

At CUNY, my experience had started out not being anything that I wanted for myself. I didn't feel like I fit in, and I wasn't feeling particularly challenged by the curriculum. It felt like the 13th grade in high school. The students were immature and so familiar — always the same faces, places, conversation, and same experiences. It was all so predictable. I wanted something different from what CUNY was offering me. I wanted to meet new people from different backgrounds, have new experiences, and hear unique stories. In my upper freshman term, I couldn't enroll for the classes that I wanted during the day as they had already filled up. So, I took an art class at night to fulfill my financial aid obligation. It turned out to be an amazing experience and I loved the energy of that evening class so much so that I enrolled in all open classes at night for my course requirements.

After a few weeks of my evening class schedule, I realized that I had all this time during the day and decided to get a job. I landed a part-time job doing administration at an employment recruitment agency. I started to make money and gain valuable work experience while I was in school. Ultimately, this was the first step in the acquisition of skills that launched my career and gave me a head start compared to all my school peers in my age group. While I was gaining the necessary work experiences and academic knowledge simultaneously, my peers were only acquiring the latter.

While I had resisted having to stay in New York and go to CUNY, I trusted the process. I let go of my resentment and decided to embrace what I had now. I was determined to make the best of the situation. It led me to new experiences that helped me grow my career exponentially. Even though I didn't get the experience of living on my own, I got hands-on work experiences that have proven to be just as, if not more, valuable.

In life, you will experience moments of doubt, resistance, and feelings of insignificance. It happens to all of us. The key is to embrace the doubt and uncertainty, yes all of it, no matter how difficult it may feel to do so at the time. This will take conscious effort and practice, but it will put you ahead of the game.

Having faith and an unwavering belief in life as it unfolds is something that I still practice to this day with deliberate effort and intention. It is not always easy. There are days when I feel like I can't get out of bed because life seems so hard. I have good days and bad days, but both require that I express an immense amount of gratitude in each moment. Sometimes these moments are large and other times they feel tiny. However, they are all significant. Some of my small moments even include struggling to wake up in the morning on weekends.

The other day, all I wanted to do was sleep in to start my weekend. I had a long and strenuous week and I felt exhausted. I was depleted — mentally, emotionally, and physically. I wanted to stay in bed with my blackout shades drawn. All I wanted was to just forget about my to-do list for the day, but I knew I couldn't do that. So, I prayed, meditated, roll-called my gratitude list, and popped myself out of bed to tackle the day. My gratitude list is a running tally of all the things, big and small, for which I am thankful. Over the years, I have come to love my gratitude list, and I see reasons to be thankful in everyday moments. Gratitude roll-calling has become a habit over the years and in quiet thinking moments, I often find myself reflecting on all the amazing things (good and bad) that have occurred in my life. It is the fact that I am truly grateful for it all that I continue to uncover greatness.

The other day I was sitting outside my home thinking about a big career decision I must make. My thoughts were distracted by a ladybug that flew and landed on my knee. I love ladybugs because I believe they bring good luck and often come to you in times of need. I was so thankful for that small moment because it took the stress out of the decision that I needed to make. The decision didn't go away but the stress and negative emotions associated with it was eliminated. It is often a series of small moments that have the biggest impact on your life. Every time I think about all the beautiful things on my gratitude list, I feel immensely happy. It gives me energy. Your gratitude list can be as small as your appreciation for a blue sky, a funny joke, or larger blessings like family, your home, and your career.

The last promise I made to my grandmother, to live my fullest life, has also instilled in me a greater commitment to trusting the process. I used to spend countless hours on all the wrong things. I would often let my inner voice take over and get the best of me. I would mull over the things that happened in the past, make up stories in my mind about why things happened the way they did, and reasons for why things weren't going my way.

I was often preoccupied with how I appeared to the world and I wanted to be sure I was projecting the appropriate story. In other words, I wanted to have the kind of story that checked all the boxes. I didn't want to be a girl lost from the hood. I did not want people to look at me and say, "See, she is just like the rest of them."

As a black woman in corporate America, I didn't want to appear as a fatherless, poor black girl who lived in public housing in Brooklyn's roughest neighborhood. I didn't want to be looked upon as someone who needed to be pitied. I felt that I was special and different, and I constantly thought about what I needed to do to appear as such to the rest of the world. I was often scared to take risks. I was calculated about everything I said or did in public, and with whom I shared intimate details of my life. I was an overachiever in both my private and professional lives and I was in constant pursuit of perfection. It took decades, in fact, most of my life, to realize that being a fatherless, poor black girl from the projects was an important part of my journey. It has shaped the person that I am today and everything about that is perfect.

The lesson I've learned from that experience is to run my race my own way and in my own time. Life is a series of unknowns, full of things that are not guaranteed. A key to a happy and successful life is less about what happens to you and more about how you choose to handle the things that life throws your way. Be grateful and be present so that you can unearth everything that is there to be learned from each of life's moments. Every human being experiences moments differently. What devastated me may not bother you in the slightest, and what doesn't impact me may be a huge burden in your reality.

There are no right or wrong answers. There is just the process, and if you don't trust it, then how will you ever get to your best life?

WHAT'S HOLDING YOU BACK?

Life coach Tony Robbins says, "If you are not growing, you are dying." I am a big proponent of that mantra and live by it. Trying new things expands every part of life. Exploring the unfamiliar and the new helps you to identify what you want to do, as well as what you don't want to do (which is just as valuable as knowing what you want) and where you want to go next in your life. This is the surest way to broaden your perspective, develop a limitless mind-set and become an expanded version of yourself.

The power of a limitless mind-set will benefit your career as well. There are plenty of ways to be unbounded and limitless in your career. Signing up to be a part of a task force on a project that stems beyond your core competency is a great way to get outside your core strengths and comfort zone. Explore new approaches to business and gain new perspectives by taking a class outside of your expertise. You could volunteer within a peer group or charity in an area that you have not worked in previously. These are just a few great ways to try something new and meet new people.

> **"If you're not growing, you're dying."**
> (Tony Robbins)

I jumped into something new a few years ago that has served me well. I took on a new job and moved across the country to Los Angeles — away from my friends, family, and all things familiar in New York City. In addition to setting up a new home and having to build a brand-new network of friends and colleagues, I also had to deal with the pressures that come along with a new leadership role. I would be leading new product portfolios, new projects, and new team members. At 38 years old, I was going to be living outside the borders of New York for the first time in my life, something I wanted to do two decades prior. This was another moment that showed me the power of trusting the timing of life. It happens when it is supposed to and in perfect orderliness.

Nevertheless, I had many moments of self-doubt and anxiety that I had to push through. When I was first offered the opportunity, I immediately wanted nothing to do with it. I was comfortable exactly where I was, and I felt safe there. I had achieved substantial success in my career, I tackled a fear and achieved my bucket list with an opportunity of a lifetime on a reality television show, and so I thought my life had launched and now it was time to simply ride the wave. Eventually, in the spirit of "Y.O.L.O." (You Only Live Once), I realized that I wanted to be true to the commitment I made a few years prior and Live My Life Out Loud. In my grandmother's eulogy, I repeatedly injected the phrase, "This ain't a dress rehearsal." In other words, life doesn't provide a do-over. You have one life. If you don't maximize it while you have it, you can never get it back. With that in mind, I agreed to take on the new role and make the move.

I knew that it was the right thing for my life and career, but I still had to work to convince myself of it every single day leading up to my move. It turned out to be one of the best decisions I have made in my life. What started out as a six-month trial eventually evolved into three-plus years of life in Los Angeles and even a promotion as the chief marketing officer of the second largest premium pH water brand in the United States. Initially, I hated L.A. I missed home, I had no rhythm, no flow, my dating experience was horrible, and it was a struggle to find my tribe. I felt like I just didn't fit in. I fought it to the end and, after 18 months in corporate housing, my feelings slowly shifted from "I can't wait to go home" to "Oh, wow, I really live here — I guess I'd better find a permanent place to live."

The key to trying new things is to get out and do it in the first place. Ask yourself, "What's holding me back? Why am I not starting?" In my experience writing this book, I stalled because I was afraid that my story wouldn't be good enough. My beliefs made me feel like I wasn't good enough and, failing at publishing this book, would prove that. I, therefore, preferred to not try in fear of failing. These negative thoughts prevented me from living out loud. And, because I wasn't fulfilling on my promise to my grandmother to live my greatest possibilities, I felt fraudulent. It was during this time that a group of wonderfully supportive friends encouraged me into diving back into writing and completing this book. I am so grateful for their encouragement, but at the end, it was me who had to push past fear and feelings of inadequacy. It will likely be challenging to push yourself to try new things, and it may not always feel right, but that's okay. New shoes can pinch for a bit before you break them in. In the same vein, new things often require pushing past your insecurities, comfort zone, and fears.

I have mentored many men and women over the years and I have observed some important differences between the two genders. One of these differences is the comfort level in trying new experiences. Men often seem to always feel ready for the next thing — the next promotion, the new challenging project the company is embarking on, management role, etc. Women, on the other hand, are more hesitant to take on what is unfamiliar to them and don't "feel ready." The thing that especially blows my mind in this is that women are almost always more qualified for the very things that they are "not ready for." We hold back when there is no reason to be afraid or hesitant.

Unlike men, most women tend to internalize their insecurities even when those insecurities are likely irrelevant to the outcome. Women are often in a state of deficit — a state of lack, feeling like they are less than, not good enough or incapable of taking on a new challenge. In one way or another, all women have feelings of uncertainty. The way to overcome this is to openly and freely talk about your beliefs, challenges, and feelings with others in your network, especially fellow women. The chances are high that the things you feel insecure about, others around you are also experiencing. Open dialogue about what's holding you back creates a supportive community around you. It is okay to get help from others, and sometimes it is necessary to do so.

I have many sounding boards in my life. I take pride and care in surrounding myself with a network of dynamic, powerful, intelligent, and successful men and women. They are like my personal trusted advisers for different areas of my life — career, spirituality, health, finances, and relationships. I go to them regularly for advice and support. Our conversations often start with, "I have this new idea," "there's an opportunity in front of me that I'm considering" and "what do you think about this?" My personal advisers help me navigate my own insecurities, moments of self-doubt and areas where I lack clarity. Peer-to-peer mentorship is a valuable tool.

There is power in numbers. Have a tribe of strong and positive family and friends in your life. Human beings need to be in the company of others, and women need other women. We need connection, comradery, and counsel to help us to think through our emotions and perspectives in various life situations. Even experiences that you do end up going through on your own can and should be shared experiences. This will help others around you grow and expand as well. Often, we think situations happen to us alone, as if they can only happen to us. The reality is that when we talk about "our independent experiences" we realize just how common most things are and the many options we can consider to resolve our issues. Do not reinvent the wheel if you don't have to. Ask others for advice and guidance and learn from the lessons of their experiences.

As you get support from your trusted community, it is

equally important to trust yourself. Human beings have the fortitude to know what is right for them. We are all guided by a higher vibrational energy that gives us signs. It is important to be present and listen for the signals from the Universe. Gut checking, as I like to call it, is a major factor in how I make decisions. My intuition is like my compass and I rely on it to show me the way. I rarely make decisions that don't "feel" right.

A woman's intuition is immensely powerful. Our soul knows what is right for us before our conscious brain becomes aware of it. Once I feel in my gut what the right decision is, I don't hold back. Ultimately, I take a pragmatic approach to how I make decisions, but I generally move on my instinct. I weigh my options including the pros and cons of each, I examine the opportunity costs of my decisions, and I assess whether the decision aligns with my morals and values. I make my evaluation and from there, trust in God and take the plunge.

Think about the things that hold you back and deal with them. We all have insecurities and we need to work through them with the powerful community of people around us. Find inspiration. Have trusted advisers in your life, but also trust yourself. Your gut and intuition are not to be taken for granted. They will guide you exactly where you need to be.

SOMEDAY MAY NEVER COME

I'm going to share with you some of the same inspiration that I have received from the amazing mothers in my life. You can have and be anything you want in life. You get to define your dreams for yourself and live the life that makes you happy and feel fulfilled.

Growing up as a child, I came from very humble beginnings. We lived in a low-income neighborhood and all around me I saw a lot of people who did not have the things they wanted in life. They were not living the life of their dreams. But my mother made sure that I grew up to believe in my dreams and to one day have all the things that I desired. She encouraged me to see beyond my current circumstances and go after what I wanted.

You already have everything you need to realize your dreams. Where most people falter (myself included) is in the waiting. We hold off on prioritizing our desires and wants to think they can be fulfilled later. People, especially women, put others first today and think that they will tend to their own needs as soon as the next opportunity to do so comes around. Here's the thing, someday may never come. Today is the only thing that is guaranteed. There have been many moments in my life where I have had to learn this lesson the hard way. I have had my own rude awakenings.

I remember 2013 only in a cloudy haze. I was beyond exhausted that entire year. I had been pulled in every single direction at once for work, I felt undervalued and that my contributions were unappreciated and, worst of all, I let myself go. I neglected myself, my needs, and my wants. My relationship status was basically non-existent. I finally removed myself from a complicated relationship with someone who was emotionally unavailable. My personal life was a hot mess because I didn't have the time or energy to get my personal priorities organized. I didn't make any time for myself. I felt depleted in every way possible. Every day I told myself that someday that year I was going to take a break and take some time out for myself. Someday I was going to "fix" me.

By the time I got a chance to take a break, it was already the end of the year. I decided that I would use the annual week-long holiday break at our company to catch up on my life, get organized and get some much-needed rest. All I wanted was to unplug from the chaos. At the last minute, just before the break, a project came up and I was sequestered into executing on it. Why? Because everyone else in the company had family commitments and being a family of one culturally meant I didn't have "a family." I was asked to drop my plans and work. What was meant to be a week where I was going to recharge and fill up the mental and emotional energy I so desperately needed to replenish, ended up depleting me even more. I felt completely insignificant. Why wasn't my family of one deemed important?

I was crushed. I had previously made myself so available to my job, that I was being counted on to work through Christmas and New Year's. So available to my job, that I wasn't focused on dating the way I should have. I wasn't prioritizing personal relationships in the way I was prioritizing work alliances. I waited for the "right" time to take a break and take care of myself and it never came. I had been looking forward to having time off the entire year and I was ultimately left in tears at the idea that I had to spend another holiday pushing through. Waiting only caused me to further neglect myself.

In 2014, shortly after my breakdown on New Year's Eve, I finally took some time out for myself. I ignored work and put it at the back of my mind. I spent some time in solitude and self-reflection. I found myself reading The Alchemist by Paulo Coelho and had my first introduction to motivational guru Tony Robbins. What these materials exposed me to made me realize that I needed to develop an action plan for my life. The plan was to prepare for today and stop waiting for tomorrow. There was only N.O.W.

There was another lesson waiting for me. I had always imagined myself having my own nuclear family as a wife and mother. At that time, I was 37 years old and had been abstinent for 1.5 years. There was no indication of a husband or children soon for me at that time. I decided that I was going to stop waiting and act. It was time to take control of my destiny. I decided to freeze my eggs. I pulled the plug on the biological clock and I had to forego any insecurities or doubts I had about not doing things the natural way. Someday was leaving me with so many uncertainties, like whether I would be able to have a baby later in life, and I was done with it. I realized that the things I wanted tomorrow required that I make some necessary decisions today.

You do not need to wait to have the things you have dreamt for yourself. In fact, you should stop waiting. Act N.O.W. and make the necessary choices today because someday may never come. Don't be left disappointed, waiting for what could be. Everything that should be is happening right now.

LIFE HAPPENS WHEN YOU ARE IN ACTION

> " Act N.O.W. and make the necessary choices today because **someday may never come.**

Taking inspiration from Newton's Laws of Physics, a body in motion stays in motion. The things you want in your life are well within your reach. In other words, lean forward, hold your hand out and grab what you want for yourself. You must act to have the kind of success and happiness that you deserve. Life happens when you are in action.

I meet a lot of people who approach me for advice. Two questions that I always ask others, and myself, are "What are your goals"? And "What's stopping you?" I will ask you the same, what are your goals? So, what's stopping you?

There is a misconception that we must have our lives

planned out and our goals are a direct reflection of a perfectly curated life. There is nothing further from the truth. Not everyone has or knows what their three-, five-, seven- or 10-year goals are. But having a plan for the things that you want to focus on, even in the immediate future, is powerful. A thought written down is an idea. An idea with a result is a goal. A goal with steps to achievement is a plan, and a plan with implemented actionable steps is all it takes to have what you want.

In 2014, I decided to have very intentional and deliberate aims. They were short-term goals for that year that I focused on every single day. There wasn't a day that I didn't work toward or think about one of my goals. AND I KEPT THEM TO MYSELF once I decided it was the right thing for me to do. My objectives that year were to:

1. Freeze my eggs.
2. Finish my manuscript.
3. Get a publicist.
4. Speak on the professional circuit about marketing and the experiences of female executives.

I physically wrote down all four of my objectives. There is immense power in putting pen to paper. Freezing my eggs wasn't even a consideration for me until I wrote it down and it became very clear how important it was to me. I encourage you to write down your own objectives on a piece of paper, and put it up somewhere in your home where you can see it every day. Spend some time each day working toward, thinking, and strategizing about the actions you will take to achieve the things that are important to you.

With intentional focus and action, I was able to achieve all my goals within the first half of the year. My eggs were frozen within six weeks after deciding, I secured my first paid speaking engagement by March, and finished my manuscript by May of that year. It was the second time I was intentional about very specific goals in my life and achieved each one of them on time. I wrote my first manuscript with a dream of publishing my own book.

Your life is too precious and your time on earth is too valuable for you to not live your fullest life. In the chaos and business of the everyday, it is easy to lose perspective on the things that matter most. It is easy to think you are acting when you are just going through the day. It is important to take a step back, reflect, and really understand if the things you do every day are contributing to the life that you deserve. Do not confuse the effort you put toward everyday tasks and activities of the ordinary life for intentional and focused work put into creating an extraordinary life. Life happens when you are in action so take measures to ensure that they are the right actions. A body in motion stays in motion. A body at rest stays at rest.

PITTMAN'S RULES:

1. Know that everything happens for a reason. You are exactly where you need to be.

2. Trust the process of life. Every moment, opportunity, challenge, and person are necessary for the lessons and blessings that are to come.

3. Seek advice from your early mentors — the women in your family who know you best. Find your tribe and create a community of trusted advisers around you, and lean on them for support. You don't have to do it alone.

4. Run your race your own way and on your own time.

5. Explore the unfamiliar. Try new things and expand your life.

6. Roll call your gratitude list.

7. Trust your intuition, and allow it to be your guiding compass.\You already have EVERYTHING you need to realize your dreams. Don't hold off on prioritizing your desires until tomorrow because someday may never come.

8. Life happens when you are in the game. Act.

9. You don't have to have it all figured out to set goals. Make short-term and immediate goals to get started, and immensely focus on them.

Chapter 2:
BE BIGGER THAN YOUR CIRCUMSTANCES

Statistically, I should not have made it and I should not have become successful. I was raised in a single-parent household by my mother. My father was not involved in my upbringing, and I barely saw or knew him. My mother and I lived in the rough neighborhood of East New York in Brooklyn. This was a place that was no stranger to murder, drugs, robberies, and poverty. Over the years, the area has seen some of the highest crime rates in Brooklyn and is considered by some to be the murder capital of that borough. The streets were deadly killing fields. Adults and children living in the neighborhood needed to be on the lookout to avoid getting involved in crossfires and getting hit by stray bullets. The conditions only further declined during the crack and heroin epidemics that impacted everyone who lived there. It was nothing less than a war zone. The life I live today is the exact opposite of the life I knew growing up. I was literally in a perpetual state of survival.

While I grew up in Brooklyn, I was actually born in Manhattan. After moving around with my mother to a few different apartments as a child, out of necessity due to difficult situations with landlords, my mother started to look for more stable, affordable and long-term housing for us. It was the 1980s, and for whatever reason, my mother and grandmother felt that housing in the projects was within our means and would give our family what we needed. They knew only what their life experiences allowed them to know and they made decisions within those parameters. My mother and grandmother felt that the projects would be the best move for my mother and me to set our roots and grow as a family.

At that time, my grandmother was working in the public sector for the city and had access to information about public housing and what was available. She came across two housing project options in Brooklyn. The first was a two-bedroom apartment in an area called Red Hook and the second option was a one-bedroom apartment in East New York in the Boulevard Houses. It was quickly decided that we would not move to Red Hook. While my mother and grandmother were not very familiar with the East New York neighborhood, what they knew about Red Hook made it an easy decision for them. Back then, Red Hook was a neighborhood that was not conducive to raising a family and, at one point, was considered the crack capital of America for the excessive use of drugs there.

My mother and grandmother took a trip — I say that loosely as they were only going to the other side of Brooklyn. They traveled east to the last stop on the Brooklyn IRT No. 3 line, to Boulevard Houses to scope out the area in person. This was a new place and a new experience for them, even though they were both Brooklyn natives. I still remember their conversation about it when they returned home later that day. They described it as feeling like they were on the other side of the world. Looking back on the moment now, I realize that they were merely working with what they knew was in their toolbox and their lens of the world was shaped by that. Taking the train to the end of the line, a bus from the train station, and then walking the three blocks it took to get to "Boulevard," as we call it, seemed like going to another country for them.

They took a chance and explored the other side of the

tracks of Brooklyn only to discover that it opened up a whole new world of opportunity for them. They saw a neighborhood that was clean and had grass, which was a big deal in the concrete jungle that is New York. They saw children playing in the parks and there were schools nearby. They were able to see me living in that neighborhood and playing in those same parks. Before they even walked into the building to see the apartment that my mother and I would potentially be living in, they were already sold on the neighborhood. It was then decided that my mother and I would move to "Boulevard" and set up our new home there.

At the time, my mother was terrified of taking a risk and being further away from my grandmother, but she moved past her fears and took a chance anyway. She took a gamble for me to give me the best life she could. This was my first exposure to risk-taking. Calculated risks are the seeds of success and my mother demonstrated that taking such measures were necessary to lead a better life. Being careful keeps you right where you are while taking a chance and making a change can take you to better places.

My mother and I settled into our new home, but things were starting to change around us. It was the mid-1980s and the landscape in the neighborhood started to decline. The year 1985 saw the introduction of the crack era and by 1989 to 1990, drugs and violence were rampant on the streets. While the housing apartment we lived in was more stable, East New York became a place of crime, poverty and marginalized communities. Education rates were low, social issues were on the rise and unemployment was high. Despite what was happening around us, my mother still took great responsibility in being charged with continuing to provide me with a safe, healthy and thriving environment in which I could grow up. She took immense measures to ensure that I was safe and secure in a neighborhood that was far from it.

As a result, I grew up in the most loving, safe and secure environment. My mother, Pamela Pittman, is my bedrock and idol. Though a young mother, she had the foresight to raise me very intentionally. From the tone of her voice, to the words she carefully chose when she spoke to me, all the way to the type of music she listened to in the house — everything was purposeful. I was the only child in the family for several years, so my family's world revolved around me. I was the apple of everyone's eye, the center of everyone's attention, the only baby in the family. I knew my mother, aunt, and grandmother would do everything they could for me and, more importantly, I knew they loved me.

So much of the confidence I have today as a grown woman stems from the love I was shown as a little girl. I grew up safe, secure and loved all while living in an urban war zone. Right outside the doors of our building, there were kidnappings, murders, crack vials littered all over the streets, and rampant prostitution and violence. It was dangerous, but I was sheltered. I had an invisible bubble around me because of my upbringing and my views on life were cheerful and optimistic despite there being so much dimness and negativity around me.

Reflecting on my childhood and my humble beginnings, I realized that they were not humble at all. I grew up in a low-income neighborhood that was rife with crime, poverty, and drugs, but that was only my circumstance. That was not my life. My mother worked very hard and sacrificed so much to give me an experience that was not what one would expect for a child growing up in the projects. She stretched our household budget in all kinds of ways to ensure that I was given experiences that were outside of my circumstances. On the one hand, we traveled to Walt Disney World four times over the course of my childhood, I went to tennis and tap lessons, and I even saw ballet shows. Meanwhile, on the other hand, I have witnessed two of my friends from school get shot and killed right in front of me as a teenager. This gave me the perspective that it was possible for my life to be different from those around me. I lived in a poor neighborhood, but I was shown what it was like to live a life that was rich of diverse experiences.

This created somewhat of a paradox, a dichotomy, a duality of reality for me between how I was being raised and the environment in which I lived. I went to school every day and I interacted with other kids who didn't have the same experiences as me. They didn't have access to the things that I had, and they weren't having the kinds of conversations at home that I was having with my mother and the rest of my family.

In our home, we talked about everything from our dreams, to our culture, to our history and so much more. Martin Luther King Jr. Day became an official national holiday in 1986, but my mother ensured that we observed that day even before it was officially recognized. My mother would stay home from work without pay and would keep me from going to school on Martin Luther King Jr.'s birthday. She made an affair of that day so that we could both honor the people who came before us and provided us with the opportunities we have today. My mother and I did so many different activities together. She would have me write book reports about African-American culture, she would read to me all kinds of incredible stories about trailblazing African-Americans in our history and we would have some of the most fascinating conversations about it all. This was not the experience that most of the other kids in school had and I was very much aware of that. I was grateful for the life that my family had made possible for me.

My mother worked tremendously hard for us and always underpinning her own work ethic, was the example she was setting for my life. She led by showing me how to live a life that was not dictated by her own circumstances. She reinforced her actions with the words she spoke to me: just because I was from it did not mean I was of it. She was unwavering in her pursuit to give me all the advantages that she could so that I could imagine a life beyond what I had as a child. She was determined to give me experiences that would make me rich in spirit so that I could have a better understanding of what my opportunities and possibilities were. I was taught very early on that my ambition always had to be bigger than my circumstances.

I remember hanging out at McDonald's with a group of my girlfriends the summer we were all between 16 and 18 years old. At this point, I was still living in Brooklyn with my mother and I was already a high school senior. We were all self-proclaimed "good girls" who stayed out of trouble and were all good students. As we chatted, the conversation moved to the topic of life after college and the career each of us wanted to have. I told my friends that I wanted to go into marketing or advertising — at the time I didn't understand the difference, and, also at that time, it was hard to differentiate between the two. One of my friends was not impressed with my choice. It wasn't a conventional career path and she kept insisting that I get clearer on the path I wanted to take. Most people who had jobs where I grew up did the work described in the title of their job. They were janitors, or postal workers, or toll booth clerks, or cashiers. These were all honorable jobs, but to say I wanted to be in marketing or advertising just didn't make sense in my world.

I didn't have a clear vision for myself at the time, but the one thing that I did know was that I was going to be making $85,000 a year by the time I was 27. To be clear, $85,000 in 1992 is the equivalent of approximately $152,000 today. This was in 1992, a time when only a few professions paid anything close to the amount that I declared I would have. My friend laughed at me and said, "Ericka, there is no way you're ever going to make $85,000 a year, let alone in 10 years!" Despite her mockery of me, I was bold, and I made a precise declaration about the future I intended to have. And just as I had declared, I made my first $87,000-income-earning year in Advertising Sales at the age of 26 as the music and entertainment manager at Vanguarde Media Inc. I asked for what I wanted, by creating a precise intention for myself, and my desire came true 10 years later.

I grew up wanting more than the kids around me. I had

big ambitions and I was proud of that. There are so many people who are uncomfortable with wanting more than those around them. They are uneasy about being ambitious. Ambition is nothing to be ashamed of. Wanting more for your life and your loved ones is a beautiful thing. When someone tells you that you can become more than you are, or shows you who you could become, believe them. If nothing else, use your own history as an indicator of the power vested within you. Examine your life and look at who you have become despite the obstacles that were placed before you. If you let your life circumstances circumscribe your ambition, then you will never truly realize all that you could have become. Had my mother not moved to the other side of the tracks in Brooklyn, her life and my life may have resulted in very different outcomes from what we have today. You cannot control the cards you are dealt in life, but you can control how you play those cards.

I am a black woman in corporate America. The intersectionality of my identity has often meant that I work in environments where barriers are put up in front of me because of who I am. I am constantly judged for the way I look. One of the biggest challenges I face is the idea that women, and often women of color, are inferior in the boardroom. I am up against this false notion, which is far from the truth, every time I take a seat at the big corporate tables. Luckily, this experience was not new to me. As a college student, my upbringing in a low-income household living in the "hood," made me feel different from most of the other students. Most people from my neighborhood did not make it to college. These experiences made me feel like I was less than those around me. These self-defeating feelings were especially prevalent in the early years of my adulthood.

In my early 20s, I was very ashamed of where I grew up. I got my first real start in my career when I joined Vanguarde Media Inc. as the music and entertainment manager. There I was exposed to a network of incredible talent, all of whom I considered superior to me in pedigree. There were a lot of rising, upwardly mobile and successful African-Americans that came from prosperous upbringings, money, and families with legacy. Each of them had a parent or two who were leaders in their industries and had phenomenal accomplishments, such as being the first African-American FBI agent in the country. While I loved being around such a dynamic group of people, I felt like I didn't belong because of where I was from. My mother worked hard and had a solid, stable, good job, but we didn't have the same kind of legacy in our family.

In sharing these feelings of mine with a mentor and dear friend Len Burnett Jr., a successful entrepreneur and a pioneer in the urban media space, I realized that I was letting my unproductive thoughts get the best of me. My mentor (and now dear friend) said, "Yes, each of us has had great legacies in our families and it is fantastic, but it is interesting that with all of the legacies, and privilege and access that we have had, somehow you are sitting at the table with us. So, what does that say about who you are if you haven't been afforded all the luxuries of life that perhaps we have? What does that say about you?"

Prior to Len sharing that perspective with me, my life and my circumstances did not occur to me in that manner. At that moment I learned that I needed to stop internalizing the thoughts and feelings that did not serve me. From that day forward, I became proud of where I came from and I am now vocal about the circumstances in which I began my life. I now share my story as a conversation starter and leave it on the table as one of the things that make me unique. Not only am I living proof that it is possible to move beyond one's circumstances, but also an example of how your circumstances can effectively prepare you for your journey as an adult.

My upbringing and the environment that I grew up in has created an immense amount of "street smarts" within me. I am practical, resourceful, I have a lot of common sense and a lot of intuition that allows me to find solutions to any problem. My childhood taught me, if nothing else, to "figure it out," on my own, even in the toughest of circumstances. My dear friend Dia Simms' mother says, "What does not knowing have to do with finding out?" I use this quote in my conversation daily. There is always a solution. During the school year, I found myself home alone every day after school ended until my mother came home from work. I was a latchkey kid for much of my childhood. From 3 p.m. to 7 p.m. I was on my own. During the summer months, I was alone from 8 a.m. to 7 p.m. Spending a lot of time by myself required me to "figure it out" and learn to navigate the neighborhood I lived in. This taught me to be resourceful and get through any situation. Living in my environment meant that I had to avoid getting kidnapped, being shot at, getting caught in the middle of a crossfire, and stumbling across drugs. Again, I was in survival mode.

As an adult and a professional, the challenges I face in the corporate world are like child's play to me because I have seen situations that are much more difficult. It is now second nature to me to navigate any complex and difficult environment in the workplace. My experiences, like learning to protect my own life and avoid getting shot at as an 11-year-old child, have made me unafraid about a lot of things in life now. I am not afraid to speak my mind, I am not timid about raising my hand and offering an alternative suggestion, and I am unapologetic about disagreeing with another person at the table. In this way, I can both command attention and demonstrate that I am a valuable member of the organization. This does not mean that I don't fight barriers, stereotypes, biases or challenges, but that I deal with them head-on.

As a strong woman of color, I often get judged by the way I look. My appearance comes with its own barriers, stereotypes, and biases that I am required to overcome. People see me, and they quickly make their own judgments about who I am, where I am from, what I know, what I don't know, how I live my life professionally and personally, and much more. Some people find it hard to believe that I used to take ballet lessons because I lived in the projects, that my mother provided a very loving home for me because she was a single mother, or that I have been to the French Riviera several times because there are not very many people who look like me out there. While I hear these comments and judgments often, they still manage to amuse me.

In the past, these misinformed assessments about who

I am used to frustrate me until I understood that I am an anomaly. I am perfectly unique. And I am enough. I don't fit the box or mold that people expect me to fit in and that's okay. I can authentically check so many boxes that, our society tells us, are reserved for people who do not look like me. And I am happy to be just the way God intended me to be, someone who cannot be pegged into a predetermined shape on the wall. I am proud to be a person who forces others to re-evaluate their stereotypes, biases, and judgments. In fact, I consider it to be my responsibility to force others to assess black women differently.

Every woman, including every woman of color, has her own story. Each of their narratives, no matter how unique, often includes experiences of being subjected to stereotypes and judgments. All women deserve to share their individual stories instead of being molded and forced into the story that others expect them to have. It is my duty, and my homage to all that my family has done for me, to share with the world all the amazing things that have happened to me to create the person I am today. The odds may have been against me, but I still succeeded. I rose above my circumstances, and I always will.

Every woman will face her own unique set of challenges, barriers, and judgments in the corporate world. Women are thriving today and our role in the workforce has evolved for the better over the years, and it will continue to do so. I believe that the next 20 years will bring with it the greatest evolution and progress made by women all around the world. It is an exciting time to be pressing for progress. The generations to come will benefit from our perseverance, just as we have benefited from the efforts of the women before us. It is for this reason that I take my position as a woman of color in corporate America so seriously. My efforts are not just to benefit me, but to leave an impact, a legacy for Millennial women and those who will come up the ranks thereafter. I am passionate about who I am and who I can be for all women. It is through this passion that I repeatedly find the fervor to push through, even the impossible, in my career.

In the various roles that I have held at Combs Enterprises, I have proven my ability to make the impossible happen, to create something out of nothing, and produce results. I make magic happen. In record time I can take an idea and turn it into a successful and thriving, tangible outcome, even when I have limited resources or knowledge about the subject matter. The results are evident in the way in which I can turn ideas into premier and number-one products, and services. That is real. My magic is real. I worked with this much impact and giving 110 percent for almost nine years at Combs Enterprises. Whether it is 5 a.m. on a Saturday or 3 p.m. on a Thursday, I expect myself to deliver every single time. My passion is not driven by the work or the products as much as my impact and what I will be known for. I want women to think about their legacy as they continue to make life decisions because each of us will have one.

Every human being has their vices and weaknesses, and I am no different. In fact, one of my biggest personal challenges is that I am a procrastinator by nature. Procrastinating makes me vulnerable to not being the best version of myself. This stems from being an overthinker, as I often want everything to be lined up the way I envision it to be for me to tackle it. The ripple effect of this is that I become easily overwhelmed when all the pieces do not align, which is often the case.

I am aware of this weakness of mine and I am present to it every time I encounter it. Acknowledging and being present to it allows me to work through it. As you work toward your own legacy, you will need to be cognizant of your own vulnerabilities and work through them. Just like your circumstances, you have the power to be bigger than your vulnerabilities as well.

MASTER YOUR INNER VOICE

We all have an inner voice that can get the best of us if we do not learn to master it. Your inner voice may tell you things like,

"You aren't enough."

"You are not deserving of this."

"Maybe you shouldn't reach so high."

"You are not ready yet."

Your inner voice is a product of, not only the collection of experiences you have had throughout your life, but also the experiences that your mother, father, and other caregivers have had in their lives. Your caregivers are your earliest influencers and their words leave a deep imprint on you. Their advice comes from their own understanding of the world, a perspective that stems from their life experiences. The words they tell you will subconsciously shape your inner voice. For me, the words that my mother and grandmother spoke to me have become the dialogue of my inner voice. They often spoke about being safe and secure. While they talked about safety and security in the context of surviving our rough neighborhoods, my inner voice has adapted this language for all areas of my life. I make many of my personal and professional decisions from the purview of safety and security. The risks that I take are almost always calculated and planned out to execution. There is often very little room for failure or letdown.

The sooner you understand how the words of your caregivers have shaped your inner voice, the sooner you will be able to master it. Self-reflect on your childhood and the priorities that your caregivers had set for you. You may choose to write down some of your memories to help you dissect and understand them. Thinking about your inner voice, particularly from the context of your ambitions, is revealing. Take a moment and examine the questions below. It may prove productive for you to jot down a few of the immediate thoughts that come up for you using the lines below. Later, take a deeper dive on these questions and try journaling about them in detail to help frame out your inner voice narrative.

What were the caregivers in your life most concerned about?

____

____

____

____

What were the beliefs and values that they most often spoke about?

____

____

____

____

What are the words that come to mind when you think about your childhood?

____

____

____

____

Take yourself back to your early years and re-create some of the moments in your mind.

Do you ever get "talked out of your ambitions"?

____

____

____

____

***What do you say to convince yourself that you cannot or should
not reach for an extraordinary outcome?***

____

____

____

____

Sometimes the words of our inner voice are loud and clear, and other times they are quiet and subtle. It is through consistent self-reflection that you will be able to discover what is stopping you. As you think about your past and present, write down the excuses that your inner voice creates to "talk you out of" your ambitions. Refer to this list of excuses to help you through times of need and moments when you lack the motivation or desire to be bigger than your circumstances. You will often find when you read out loud the list of things that hold you back that they are relatively false. Once you shift your beliefs about your life your values change and from there your actions fall in line accordingly.

The victory is in mastering your inner voice and getting out of your head. I learned this the hard way after letting my own thoughts get the best of me. For years I managed to create stories about how the world saw me, and what it might see in me. In my own private musings, I focused on what I was not, why I was not going to make the cut, and why I was not good enough. This led to a mind-set that was ultimately stalling my growth and my success. My response to this unproductive and disempowered way of being was to do everything in my power to create a narrative that was going to counter the voice that told me I wasn't enough. I began to become obsessive about becoming "perfect." I thought if only I could perfect my speech, perfect my grades, have perfect posture, and on and on the list went. One disempowered way of being ultimately led me to another self-defeating state because I was pursuing perfection when no such thing exists. I have now come to realize that I am enough, and I am perfect just the way I am.

Coming to know that I am just as I should be has been a personal journey of acceptance, patience, and self-love. Every day I repeat to myself, "I am perfect exactly as I am today, and tomorrow I get to be someone else. There is beauty in both." Giving myself permission to be just as I am while allowing myself to change and evolve has been life-changing for me. Wholeness comes from within. Knowing who I am, including my weaknesses and insecurities, has created a completeness within me that has helped me to value myself. There is a certain humbling gentleness that comes with accepting your shortcomings and knowing that they make you perfect. In accepting all of who I am, it has allowed me to find inner peace. Make no apologies to yourself about who you are. I am enough and so are you.

Mastering your inner voice is about taking control of how you speak to yourself, as well as how you hear the words of those around you. If you allow it, your inner voice will internalize the thoughts that do not serve you and turn them into a negative dialogue. I have encountered this experience throughout my life.

In my late 30s, I made the decision to extend my reproductive options by freezing my eggs. I was so proud and excited about what I had done. I wanted motherhood and I had taken the steps to keep that option open for myself in the future. I felt that was a responsible and mature decision to make and I was grateful to have the means and options available to make this choice. I couldn't wait to tell those around me about this tremendous gift that I had given myself. As I shared my exciting news, I was completely unprepared for the negative comments that I received. I heard comments like, "are you sure you want to share that news with people?" and "don't tell that to too many people, it makes you seem so old, having to save your eggs." These comments were hurtful, and they developed a self-defeating inner dialogue within me. It took me time to control my inner voice and protect it from being influenced by the words of those around me. I can't stop the world from judging me, but I can stop me from judging myself. I needed to do what was within my control and forget the rest. I was not going to let the world define my decisions.

Own your vulnerability, then move past it.

There's real power in being able to own your vulnerability and embrace it. At its core, vulnerability is about unapologetically being yourself around anyone and everyone. This was an important lesson that I learned later in my life as I wasn't vulnerable in my early years. For me, not being vulnerable came from wanting to be perfect. I felt that I needed to put my best and most proper self out into the world and save the rest of me for those I'm closest to. I wanted to reserve parts of me out of fear of being judged or being misunderstood.

I used to think that there was a perfect image for the way professionals should look and the way they should conduct themselves. I thought that my way of being needed to be aligned with the way the mainstream looked and behaved. Whether it was the way I dressed or the way I led my team, I held back for many years because I couldn't be vulnerable and share all of me just as I am. Over the years, I have come to realize that being vulnerable just allows you to connect with people on a real level and human connection is powerful equity. Not being vulnerable meant that I was not being my authentic self. This was causing me to miss powerful human connections. It wasn't about me being judged or not, but it was about me being real and sharing with the world all that I am. Allowing myself to own my vulnerability and be myself led to one of the most rewarding decisions of my life — taking part in the filming of The Singles Project on Bravo TV.

A friend of mine heard about the show and encouraged me to audition to be a part of the cast. If I were chosen to be one of six featured singles in New York City, a camera crew would follow me around for eight to 12 weeks documenting my quest to find love. Against my normal judgment, I auditioned, and I was chosen to be one of the six singles on the show. Being filmed all day and every day for 12 weeks meant that there would be no ability for me to hide parts of me or be anything but my vulnerable and authentic self. This was a stretch for me, but it was an incredible experience that helped me understand that vulnerability is a powerful tool. For the first time in my life, I showed my softer side to those outside of my closest circle.

As a leader, I now take comfort in being my authentic self around my team. I love hip-hop and R&B music and I am comfortable sharing that side of me at work. My team would not be surprised to find me bumping to music by rappers Yo Gotti or ASAP Ferg in my office while I'm working. They know that I expect the best and my energy is intense when we need to deliver. However, they also know that I am playful and fun even in those moments of stress and action. It isn't uncommon to find me problem-solving and correcting work one minute and then bursting into song and dance the next. I am just as comfortable wearing a casual blush pink romper to the office as I am wearing an all-black power suit. While both are different expressions of me, I am the same woman and the same leader in both scenarios.

Being your authentic self is the ultimate expression of vulnerability. It is not about airing out your dirty laundry or publicly crying. It is about being comfortable with yourself and with all the things that make you different. Own your uniqueness, share it with the world unapologetically and then move past it. Life is too short to be one-dimensional.

> "You get in life what you have the courage to ask for."
> (Oprah Winfrey)

Having it all means different things to different people. There is no right or wrong path. There simply is what you want and that is all the validation you need. Never be ashamed of what you want in your life. Women, more often than men, do not ask for the things that they want. While this is changing and getting better with each generation of women, the evidence between men and women in this regard is still apparent everywhere from the classroom to the office. We need to define our dreams, understand their scale and embrace them in their entirety. It was through my mother and grandmother that I learned to dream and be intentional about what I wanted. They taught me to be (cautiously) fearless in my pursuit of the life that I wanted, and I now approach every area of my life in this way.

Previously I had held the role of vice president of Blue Flame Agency with Combs Enterprises. This opportunity came because of me asking for what I wanted. After setting up a time to meet, I had an informational interview with a former chief marketing officer of Combs Enterprises at that time. We talked about our experiences and had a detailed exchange about what my next dream job could look like.

I shared with this executive what I wanted to do, what I didn't want to do and why I was deserving of exactly what I wanted. After I had prescriptively detailed my ideal role, she bought into it and told me that my vision precisely aligned with a position she was thinking of developing at the Blue Flame Agency. It was an incredible and career-altering moment for me. While serendipity played a part in obtaining this role, it would not have happened if I didn't have the courage to share what I wanted and why I was deserving of it. It is not just important to be prepared when opportunity strikes, it is also necessary to speak your desires into reality. There is power in your thoughts and there is power in your words.

Sometimes we do not ask for what we want because we don't know what we want or what is available to us. As a child, I only knew what my family shared with me and they only shared what they knew. To be courageous in my requests of what I wanted for myself, I had to first understand the possibilities that were open to me. I learned so much from my mother, aunt, and grandmother but I needed to learn from others as well. I went out and spoke to people from various backgrounds with various interests. I was able to learn about new possibilities by learning more about a variety of different people. Creating a larger and powerful network around me was critical in curating the life that I wanted.

Over the course of my life, I have surprised myself many times at all the things I was able to accomplish just by being brave enough to ask for what I wanted. Having graduated from high school early and entering college at a young age, I decided that I wanted to get my bachelor's degree and pay for it on my own. My mother provided an incredible life for me and I had never had to take on such a large expense prior to that. I wasn't sure how I was going to accomplish it, but I didn't let that stop me from having the courage to ask for what I wanted. My mother had been the sole breadwinner in our home my whole life and I didn't want to burden her with the financial responsibility of my formal education, too. Instead of partying all night like most college kids, I set financial goals for myself and created a plan that had me working during the day and studying at night. Despite having self-doubts, I successfully completed my degree, worked the entire time, and paid for my education on my own.

Be courageous in what you ask of others and what you ask of yourself. I spent many years putting other people and other things ahead of myself. From sacrificing my health and well-being to get the job done to skipping out on time for myself to be with family and friends, I fell into the pattern of making myself priority number two. This changed when I finally decided to be audacious and require myself to do what was best for me. Once I started to make myself a priority, I felt more alive and bigger opportunities started to present themselves to me. I learned that self-sacrificing was not the answer to success, and that doing so only resulted in a subpar life.

Throughout your life, you will face the barriers and the limitations of your circumstances. But that is not an excuse or a reason not to succeed. You must rise above. Your circumstances are not your fault, but if you let them dictate your outcome, then that IS your fault. Master resilience and grit and learn to navigate the waters of uncertainty. Always go headfirst into the roles, conversations, and places you need to go by stepping up and asking for what you want. Show the world your authentic and vulnerable self, and the inner voice in your mind that has the potential to shape, alter and control you. Excuses keep you exactly where you are today.

What happened in your past has nothing to do with the future chapters of your life. Your family may explain your journey, but they do not dictate your path. They do not define you.

Learning to embrace the elements of your past and having the clarity to be able to laugh at yourself will free you. You are the narrator of your life. Regardless of how your story started, you get to decide how it ends.

PITTMAN'S RULES:

1. Calculated risks are the seeds of success. Not taking a chance will keep you right where you are.
2. Make yourself a priority. You will be all the more happy and successful for it.
3. Learn to laugh at yourself, including the things that the world around you says are wrong about you.
4. Don't be afraid to raise your hand and speak.
5. Just because you are from it does not mean that you are of it.
6. Don't be ashamed of your past circumstances. They have made you who you are today.
7. Don't be so hard on yourself. Learn to master your inner voice.
8. Be vulnerable and let the world see who you really are. Let your personality shine, and share your story. People will love you all the more for it.
9. Ask for what you want in life and be unapologetic about it.
10. Always be bigger than your circumstances.

Chapter 3:
TAP INTO YOUR FEMININITY

No matter where you are in your life and career, your identity as a woman will always remain. I have spent my entire personal life and corporate career embracing my womanhood. Why? Because embracing my womanhood and my feminine energy has made me a powerful force in life, boardrooms, and important circles. And it can make you a powerful force as well.

I am unapologetically feminine in the work environment. Being a female is a powerful differentiator in a room full of "suits and ties." I have mentored many women of all ages throughout my career and I have often found that many of them consider being female to be negative to their career. They consider their womanhood as a barrier, impacting their ability to achieve power, leadership, and success in their career. I have experienced the very opposite of that in my own professional life. Being a woman has made me stand out from the pack and has provided a platform for me to be evaluated for the value of my contributions. The bottom line is, if I can show up with my feminine qualities and be better, faster, more agile, and more adaptable than the rest of the pack, everybody will notice me. Taking ownership of being a woman creates an advantage that offers something new that is missing in many boardrooms.

Young women are exposed to femininity and sexuality at opposite levels. While femininity is less apparent in everyday life, sexuality is thrown in women's faces constantly. Sexuality is rampant in advertising, social media, entertainment, and more. There is an overexposure to sexuality because sex sells, and therefore, it has also overshadowed femininity. For these reasons and more, young women are not being taught what femininity truly is. As a child growing up in the 1980s, I saw firsthand how women were encouraged to suppress their core womanliness in the business world.

The 1980s was a decade when women were moving out of "pink collar" jobs, like secretarial and retail work, in large numbers and into the workforce that had been dominated by men. Women were, largely for the first time, moving in the same circles and spaces as men. It seemed that nobody, including fashion designers, really knew how to react to this influx and sudden change. I saw working professional women being portrayed in media wearing boxed, extremely structured, broad-shouldered, masculine suits, and suspenders. There were a lot of striped suits, and the choice of footwear was wing-tipped shoes that looked more like men's dress shoes than anything else. This portrayal translated into "the fashion trend" and became the way working women dressed. It was almost as if women needed a uniform that replicated men's style and that women needed to embody masculinity to fit into the workplace. This further engrained a perspective that sexuality was still desirable for women while femininity was deemed as something that could not coexist with masculinity.

There is a heightened awareness of what sexuality is in our society and far less awareness of what femininity is. By not talking about and exposing young women to femininity, and the power within it, we don't equip them with the ability to effectively tap into their femininity. I was fortunate enough to be exposed to the power of femininity at a very early age.

By observing my grandmother, mother, and aunt while growing up, I became very clear about femininity and sexuality. Each of these three women were all working professionals who had successful careers. Watching how they operated in the world and how the world responded to them has always intrigued and inspired me. I saw the power in their presence and how they harnessed that influence to achieve their goals. They weren't proud or boastful, but powerful nonetheless. They used grace, poise, manners, and patience to serve them well over the years.

My grandmother was a middle management executive, my mother was a manager for the New York City Department of Education, and my aunt was an auditor for the National Teachers Associates Life Insurance Company. I often watched each of these incredible women get dressed for work and I observed their demeanor and the way they carried themselves. My grandmother and mother were early risers who usually started their day at 5 a.m. As a small child, I would wake up early and walk around the house following my grandmother while she got ready for work. After she put on her makeup, set her curls and got dressed in her silk blouse and wool suit, we would sit at the table and eat breakfast together. My mother took after my grandmother as she, too, always started the day by spending quality time with me. We would sit at the table and eat an awesome breakfast together that my mother lovingly prepared. Even on the days when I was off from school and did not wake up early, my mother would leave pancakes in the toaster oven for me along with the sweetest notes. They always made quality time for family while simultaneously excelling in their careers.

They embodied femininity in the most powerful ways.

The way in which I tap into the power of my femininity is a learned behavior that I attribute to my earliest mentors, the matriarchs of my family. They showed me the power and mystique in simply just being a woman. What I learned at home about femininity, combined with what I learned in entertainment about sexuality, helped me understand the difference between the two and the purpose each of them serves.

My reference to sexuality is not related to inappropriate conduct, although many women unfortunately experience this. There have been times when men, usually peers or members of middle management, have made inappropriate verbal advances at me and I have had to course-correct immediately to prevent it from getting further. I have never once thought, "Maybe I should use my sexuality to get ahead here." The reality is that word travels fast and it is more valuable for you to have substantial relationships than to have substantial knowledge. People who can advance your career can often be more concerned about what is said about you than what you know. An important part of having the kinds of relationships in which people speak highly of you is in having the utmost professionalism and protecting your reputation.

To be clear, femininity is a mind-set and a way of being. It's a combination of personality, emotion, and character. On the other hand, sexuality is an expression of your physicality. It is how humans express their intimate emotions. It is crucial that women understand the difference between the two. One is not better than the other, but they need to be used in their own unique way. If used the wrong way, sexuality can become something totally different in the work environment. There are distinct attributes, like patience and empathy, which are considered feminine. These, when used, are powerful and highly effective in the personal and professional spheres of your life. When I'm in a room full of masculine energy and I bring a feminine perspective combined with the assertiveness of my alpha roots, I find my happy space. I have learned to use the various elements of my feminine energy in highly effective ways and you can, too. Here are some of the strongest characteristics that come naturally to feminine energy that will serve you well in the workplace:

MULTITASKING

This is the ability to manage and execute multiple tasks at the same time. Life and work happen on their own terms. Sometimes when it rains, it truly does pour. Women have the added advantage of being prepared to tackle these moments because we have a natural ability to multitask. The classic image of a woman preparing dinner while carrying a young child on her hip and also helping the older child with their homework is the reality in many homes. Growing up in a single parent household, I watched my mother expertly juggle multiple responsibilities and tasks. We were blessed that my mother's work was very supportive of her responsibilities as a parent. I often went to work with her in the summers and saw firsthand how she effectively handled her assignments and managed her workflow. She was upbeat about any assignment given to her and she was meticulous and diligent about her work. She was also the woman who prepared a home-cooked dinner for us every day. In the summer months, she would cook a full meal for our dinner early in the morning before leaving for work because she didn't like "slaving over a hot stove" in the hot afternoons. My mother did it all.

In my career, I am relied on to multitask to get things done. As a chief marketing officer, I oversee large projects with various moving parts. There is always an incredible team that supports me, but I am ultimately accountable for the finished products. I recently led the development of a series of women empowerment brunches sponsored by one of Combs Enterprises' products, Cîroc Ultra Premium Vodka. These events were held in several cities around the U.S. and remarkable women were honored for their achievements. Like all other projects, there were many components to this one and we had an entire team supporting it.

I led for the most part as a macro manager because I believe that I have the right people in place to do their jobs and I trust them to do it well. However, on the day of each of the events, I am on the ground checking all the boxes to make sure people have done their jobs, I am providing advice and coaching to staff, problem-solving when issues occur, checking in on attendees, and sometimes even preparing an impromptu opening address that I hadn't prepared for. I am a natural at juggling multiple tasks and in this way, I am not an anomaly. Modern day women are skilled at multitasking.

Working in high-intensity environments has forced me to become even more proficient at multitasking. I am constantly managing conference calls, approving marketing creatives, signing off on expenses, reviewing pitch proposals and editing videos in a two-hour window during my work day. My personal life is also very full. I am constantly managing photoshoots, presenting at speaking engagements, assessing my personal finances and investments and juggling household responsibilities. To add to this, I regularly travel back and forth between my home in Los Angeles and my home in New York. I have come to lovingly rely on my calendar and the reminders that it sends to my phone to help keep me on track and ahead of the game.

BEING NURTURING

There is a misconception that being nurturing equates to "mothering" people, being soft-spoken or even being a pushover. I am none of those things, but I am still a nurturing leader. I am assertive, I make sure people hear me when I speak, and I am most definitely not easily fooled or told what to do. Being nurturing is to support, encourage and develop your team to perform at their best because, when they perform at their best, you as a leader will also perform at your best. Women are some of the most naturally nurturing leaders and the world needs more of us.

While I am a perfectionist and like to see "perfect" results, I trust each of my team members to fulfill their responsibilities with quality and care. I take the time to clearly communicate my expectations and ensure that everyone is sure of their responsibilities and their role. Each member of my team is treated with the same respect that I expect for myself. When a mistake is made, I approach it with optimism, compassion and laughter — mistakes are expected. I don't dwell on the errors, but I do acknowledge the breakdowns, ensure that I course correct immediately and clearly communicate that the same mistake should not be repeated in the future. I want each of my team members to succeed with or without me and that is real power.

An important part of being nurturing is to nurture a situation instead of just steamrolling ahead into it. Operating from a space of compassion is important and can help you to nurture a situation, even the difficult ones. When you take an empathetic approach to a situation and tap into the hurdles that the people involved may be experiencing, you can identify solutions that positively impact everyone involved. When everyone wins, we can all be happier. This will reflect in your results as well.

SOLUTIONS-FOCUSED

I am always problem-solving. My team looks to me for advice and input and I always show up for them ready to lead. They feel safe coming to me with a problem because I focus on what is most important — the solution. Being solution-focused is to think about the solution and not the problem, focus on the strengths and not the weaknesses, and the desired end-result instead of the root cause. Being in this frame of mind allows me to create a safe space where my team feels comfortable approaching me and ensures that I find answers even when I have little to no knowledge about a subject-matter.

I believe, as Sheila Banks always says, that not knowing the answer has nothing to do with finding out what it is. That is why I am rarely in a position where I don't know the answer. When I don't have a solution, my response is always, "Let me find out for you." Sometimes this means that I am asking somebody else for the answer, doing research, or thinking back into my past experiences for a guiding compass. This does not mean that I am accountable for everyone's job and responsibilities but that I can provide solution-focused leadership no matter what the situation is. I set this tone for my team for when the question comes up about how to do something that we've already discussed — I expect them to have the answer. If the question ever comes up, my expectation is that there is someone who will have the answer. It is just a matter of searching to figure it out.

BEING EMPATHETIC

Everyone has their own story, their own perspectives, and their own feelings. There is immense power in being able to understand what another person is going through, even when you haven't experienced it yourself. When you can see things from someone else's frame of reference, you can better connect with them and therefore, more effectively support them. Women are powerful leaders because we are better able to provide the right advice, coaching, and guidance for each unique individual.

Showing another person that you understand what they are dealing with, and you are willing to support them in that, fosters an opportunity to work together effectively. Successful team builders are very high on the empathy scale because they listen, understand and they care. The character trait of empathy is a positive attribute that allows women to be inclusive in decision-making, problem-solving, and creating an open dialogue within the team environment. We are not just interested in our own opinions but also see value in the thoughts shared by others.

FINDING CONSENSUS AROUND THE TABLE

In a group setting, having the ability to look at a situation from everybody's viewpoint and then identifying a win-win not only earns the respect of everyone at the table but also gives you an advantage. There is a level of diplomacy that is required to create a consensus within a team successfully and, it is not that men do not have the ability to lead in this way, it just doesn't come to them naturally. If there are 12 men in the room and you are the only woman there, use your ability to find consensus to help everyone involved in the conversation win. Your ability to triumph faster than the men will make you stand out. They will be left wondering, "Wow, how did she get a win for everybody? How did she do that?"

My feminine energy and the value it brings to the table is one of the reasons why I am confident being in a boardroom full of men while donning a pair of stilettos and a well-fitted dress. It is why I don't have to compromise my style or leadership presence - allowing me to be poised and primped all at the same time. While they are very powerful traits, femininity is also more than only multitasking, being nurturing, having a solutions-focused approach, being empathetic, and having the knack to find consensus around the table. Femininity is also being compassionate, having patience, grace, poise, resilience, and more. These are not traits that are exclusive to women, but in my experience, they come more naturally to us.

My power comes in knowing that I naturally possess these traits and abilities and tapping into them. The notion that these feminine traits are obscure to effective business dealings is a myth and it is rather the contrary. If you want proof look no further than Combs Enterprises, where there have been a significant number of female executives in senior leadership team over the years. With an ever-strengthening suite of brands that have become household names and rising profits, the results are a clear indication of the power of femininity in the board- room.

The other big myth about femininity is that it presents a weakness. In 2016, at The Chicago Network`s 27th Annual Women in the Forefront Luncheon, Ariel Investments` president Mellody Hobson spoke about the one thing she is trying to leave with people — being brave. She eloquently said, "To be brave and not allowing things to happen to you. To not be at the effect of the world. To control your own destiny. To be brave in speak- ing your truth. To be brave in controlling your own destiny. To be brave in trying to do the impossible. And when you are brave, you feel fear. You know, your chest is a little tight and you're nervous or sweaty or whatever it might be. It all affects us in different ways. But you cannot be brave without fear."

The gentleness of femininity at the surface level may be misinterpreted as being weak, meek, or docile when that is not true. It is perhaps the subtlety of femininity that gives it the most power. It is this perceived "weakness" that in fact allows us, women, to bring our femininity through the door and disarm aggressive and difficult situations so effectively. My only wish is that I understood the incredible power of femininity and how to leverage it in my career sooner. To be feminine will require you to be brave. You will feel fear but follow that fear and let it guide you. That is where your truth can be found.

In the beginning, I did not know the immense power that femininity would have on my career. While I had incredible women in my life who taught me what femininity was, I did not know how to apply it. My pitfall for not realizing this sooner was that I was groomed by male mentors for most of my professional life. All the tools and skills I had developed were derived from discussions about male success stories. I utilized their wins as examples of how to succeed and applied that lens to navigate my own leadership journey. My male mentors have been so important to my career, but they just couldn't tell me about the things that they did not know and being a woman in business was one of those things. It wasn't until I had hit a wall in my professional growth that I discovered some of the missing pieces in who I was being and what I was presenting at work.

I found myself suffering from extreme communication gaps in my peer groups and interactions with my team members. While I was respected by most, it was clear that I was not liked by many, and the reality was that people often wanted to do business with those who they liked. People like people who are like them. This had become problematic for me and was causing my results to plateau. My professional demeanor can feel polarizing for some people. I am always prepared, well-spoken and buttoned up. I received executive coaching when I first started in my role as the vice president of the chairman's office at Combs Enterprises.

The coaching was important for my new role in providing a full understanding of how people in the organization perceived me, up until that point, to determine the areas that I needed to improve on. The resounding theme from the evaluations about me from my colleagues and peers was that I was too professional. One individual even said, "She makes you feel like you have to get dressed for court and have an attorney represent you." The feedback was that I needed to show more of my personality to others and conduct myself in a different way so that my colleagues could feel safer around me. This is when I realized that I needed female mentors to talk to.

How were other women effectively balancing between being unapologetically themselves while being likable? Women like hip-hop sensation Cardi B and political commentator, attorney and principal and CEO of IMPACT Strategies Angela Rye have succeeded in closing the communication gap. Angela Rye discussed this very topic in an interview with Refinery29 saying, "I feel like the best thing that I can do to liberate black women and women of color is to be my unapologetic self. I feel like we have carried the burden of making people comfortable for too long, at the risk of our own comfort and physical and emotional health. And ain't nobody got time for that. If being myself makes you uncomfortable, well, that's just too damn bad." I wanted to learn from other powerful women, so I sought female mentors.

WHY EVERY WOMAN MUST HAVE FEMALE MENTORS

I discovered that, as I was growing in my career, I needed guidance on harnessing my femininity, something I was gravely lacking for many years. I would walk into high-intensity board meetings like a bull in a fine china shop (or so I've been told, verbatim) — stern, assertive and aggressive — because that is what my male mentors had taught me to do for years. I have heard many times in my life, "what is good for the goose is good for the gander"- unfortunately all things in business are not created equal. At some point, this strategy was not always serving me well and I learned how to finesse my approach from incredible women like Suzanne de Passe.

Suzanne was, and still is, an acclaimed media juggernaut. Her awards and accomplishments range from receiving multiple Emmy Awards to an Academy Award nomination, and her diverse portfolio spans from everything from being an executive producer for television shows to being the president of Motown Productions. We hit it off early on and developed a great relationship. It was uncanny the similarities in our professional experiences. She had a close working relationship with Berry Gordy, founder of Motown Records, and I with Sean Combs at Combs Enterprises. I am grateful that she has given me access to her immense knowledge and vast experiences. My female mentors, like Suzanne, taught me that being feminine is not a sign of weakness. They helped me understand that gender differences are empowering disruptors to what we traditionally see in the corporate world. Women have the ability to contribute to conversations in a fresh and new way that is needed. The feminine energy was a new wave in leadership consideration and my female mentors taught me how to be a part of this wave and push to break the glass ceiling. They taught me how to effectively harness the feminine energy that my earliest mentors displayed every single day.

For the Women in the Workplace 2017 report co-developed by LeanIn.org and McKinsey & Company, a comprehensive study was conducted to examine the state of women in corporate America. Researchers analyzed human resources data from 222 companies that employed more than 12 million men and women. The data showed that women continue to remain underrepresented at every level in corporate America, despite being more highly educated than men. The study also found that mentorship had a clear benefit for career progression, but women received less of it than men. While this is the general reality for women, it does not have to be your reality. A company-sponsored mentorship program is not the only avenue to find mentors. Seek advice and guidance from those around you, including your peers. Peer mentorship is how some of the most successful women ban together to break the glass ceiling.

For their 2018 #InItTogether initiative to celebrate women, Issa Rae, an American actress, writer, director, producer and web series creator, partnered with LinkedIn. In an interview in support of the initiative, Issa Rae spoke about the impact that powerful peer mentors in the entertainment industry had on her career. Women like Ava DuVernay, Shonda Rhimes, and Mara Brock Akil encouraged her to say "no" and speak up for herself, something that she had not done throughout her corporate career. By hearing the personal stories they shared, Rae found the courage to say "no" herself and now imparts the same advice to other women in the industry.

Mentors can come from anywhere. They could be your teachers, people you read about, people you see on television, your bosses, and so much more. However, in my experience, your earliest mentors are the ones that come from home. They are your family members that have shaped you and for me, they were my grandmother, my mother, and my aunt. These were the women who I posed my burning childhood questions to, they were the ones who I sat down with to chat about anything without concern, and they were also the ones who so eloquently modeled the kind of woman I should grow up to be.

My mother is my definition of ultimate femininity. She has a personality that makes her a force to be reckoned with. She can be direct and aggressive when she needs to be, but she primarily operates from a very understanding, supportive, neutral and diplomatic space. She remains in that cadence no matter what challenge she is confronted with. She doesn't show emotion quickly and she is very level-headed when she thinks through solutions. My mother smiles nicely but not softly. She is by no means a soft woman, but she is a gentlewoman. My grandmother was much like my mother, both strong-willed but very sophisticated in their mannerisms.

From the time I was little, my grandmother encouraged me to be who it was I wanted to be. She pushed me to try new and unfamiliar things just as she had. She spoke her mind and had my back when I bravely thought for myself. In fact, she always applauded me when I wasn't shy in expressing my thoughts, even if others weren't quite prepared to hear it. As a young woman starting out in the business world, I had the confidence to make hard decisions and share my thoughts because I knew that, no matter what I did, however right or wrong it was, there were always people who had my back. My grandmother taught me to be all these things but to do so with the kind of poise and sophistication that comes from feminine energy. Our early mentors are crucial for success and building the courage to be ourselves.

What is important, however, is to continue to find new role models as you move through life just as I had. By finding new female mentors, I was not replacing or displacing my loved ones, but rather complementing the things that they had already taught me. You need new mentors throughout your life because new life situations, challenges, and goals also require new information. You can take the values your caregivers taught you at the kitchen table into the boardroom, but how to best apply those values with integrity in a corporate setting requires a nuanced understanding of your industry and profession.

A CASE FOR FEMININITY

Women possess distinct feminine qualities which can and should be used as an asset in business. Taking ownership of being a woman creates an advantage. It disrupts the status quo and the way of operating in the "boys' club," a model of operation that is all too common in many workplaces. Femininity is the ability to influence without artifice. It is a warm and welcoming way of being that creates a positive space for all those touched by it. Feminine energy is rooted in power and leadership that, when harnessed and utilized authentically and accurately, it can command presence.

All women have this immense power within them and the key is in learning how to leverage it effectively. In recent years, I have learned the subtle art of leading with my femininity. The result has been profound. You must learn to use your femininity effectively because, when it is used effectively, it can be a potent business tool.

I have been able to create a more inviting space for people to get comfortable with all the things that make up my personality and leadership style. It has served me very well in making alliances in business as my feminine energy complements my overall personality.

I was cast for Bravo TV's show The Singles Project, a dating show to capture the New York City dating scene for young professionals. While reality TV was completely outside of my comfort zone, I decided to be a part of it to show women around the world another aspect of effectively leading as a woman. The show allowed me to exemplify an alternative representation of women of color within media and entertainment and how we portray our feminine energy, illustrate that women are multidimensional and dynamic with our feminine qualities, and use my experiences on the show to fuel dialogue to further empower women. Being on the show also allowed me to show women around the world what it looks like for a professional woman to lead with feminine energy in dating. I met a great guy in the long run, but more importantly, I was able to show women the power of being a woman. Femininity is a force in the professional world, in dating, and in friendships.

My friendships are a significant part of my happiness and success. My chosen family consists of six girlfriends who are like sisters to me. We have a friendship that is unbreakable and has been as such through all stages of our lives, even when we have ventured on different paths. We have an unspoken rule that we will always be there for each other and lift each other up higher as women. Our bond is so strong because we lead with our feminine energy in our friendship. We are kind and supportive of each other, we are empathetic to each other, and we support one another unconditionally. Femininity has been a powerful force for me. Hold onto your femininity, assign it the true value it deserves in all areas of your life, and celebrate it out loud.

"THE MICHELLE OBAMA EFFECT"

A woman who embodies feminine energy powerfully is the former first lady Michelle Obama. When I think of the former first lady, the first words that come to my mind are femininity and power. She is not vulnerable, something that some people have attacked her for, and does not display emotions in public but she is a force. Being a first family in the White House for eight years has meant that her relationship with her husband was, and still is, in the public eye. Her marriage with former president Barack Obama created a narrative around her that almost softened her and brought a gentleness to her.

She has created a space in her marriage that has allowed her husband to embody his masculine energy. When you see them together he can be found being flirtatious with her, the two of them being physically affectionate with each other, and we get glimpses of them sharing an emotional moment where she softens up and is gentle. You see this side of Michelle Obama when she is with her children as well. She is affectionate, kind and loving with her two daughters. Her feminine energy has been brought to the forefront in many ways and none of those ways has compromised the power that she holds. There isn't anything soft about Mrs. Obama in politics and business. She is a force, 100 percent alpha. My view of her is one of the strongest leaders and as someone who leverages her femininity effectively.

Using your femininity on a personal level, like Michelle Obama, is the same as using it professionally but also different. On a personal level, everybody needs their sexuality and, while I can not speak intelligently on multidimensional gender roles, I can say for heterosexual traditional relationships I've found that for women they also need to use their femininity to complement the masculine energy of those in their lives. A woman must be feminine if she wants her man to be masculine.

She may want to allow him to lead if she wants him to make leadership decisions in the relationship. It is important for women to be mindful of if and how they embody masculine energy in their intimate relationships because a woman's masculine energy will compete with a man's masculine energy if she is not careful. If a woman comes from feminine energy than that will perfectly complement a man's masculine energy. This is not about being inauthentic, or subservient, but it is about allowing your partner the space to be who he needs to be in order to complement the relationship. It appears, Michelle Obama has mastered her ability to let her husband be the kind of person he needs to be to complement her instead of competing with her.

I learned to apply, what I am coining as "the Michelle Obama effect" at Combs Enterprises when I worked with Sean Combs because he has a very strong masculine energy. He is very alpha and is a force. I realized that in working with him closely that oil and fire only make an explosion. In other words, I needed to learn to complement his masculine energy and become fluid with my energy for us to work together harmoniously and cohesively. I had to heighten my feminine energy to align myself with him. As a result, we achieved tremendous professional success.

I often talk to women I mentor about femininity versus sexuality because it is so important to understand how to utilize each one separately. They are both powerful and are equally ours to possess and use as we desire. However, there is far more untapped strength in femininity than there is in sexuality. We need to have more dialogue about femininity and teach young women how to harness it effectively for success professionally and personally.

PITTMAN'S RULES:

1. Femininity and sexuality are equally powerful but distinctly different. Learn to use each one as it should be used.
2. Be unapologetically feminine. It will make you stand out.
3. Protect your reputation at all costs — otherwise, it will cost you.
4. Learn to effectively use the various elements of your feminine energy. You will be all the more successful because of it.
5. Femininity is not a weakness. Do not misinterpret its gentleness for a loss of power.
6. Always have female mentors who can guide you in effectively leveraging your femininity.
7. Do not forget your earliest mentors, the women who have been in your life from the beginning.
8. Harness the power of femininity in your professional and personal lives, including your friendships.
9. Employ "the Michelle Obama effect" in your personal life. Being feminine in your marriage or partnership is not a sign of weakness.
10. Talk about femininity so that we can help all women effectively tap into the power of theirs.

Chapter 4:
NEVER LOSE YOUR CHILDLIKE WONDER

The human spirit is a miraculous and resilient thing. We have infinite potential and can fulfill all possibilities. If harnessed and used correctly, the human spirit can take you places you never dreamed you could go.

At the age of 5, my sister, mother, grandmother and I took a family vacation to Walt Disney World in Orlando, Fla. This was in the early 1980s, the time when Disney Imagineers were building a new theme park called the Experimental Prototype Community of Tomorrow, also known as the EPCOT Centre. At that time, this park was destined to be the "wave of the future" and was a technology-themed park. During our family vacation, the park was still under construction, but it was so revolutionary that Disney decided to open it up to the public before completing it. Park visitors were given the opportunity to experience the EPCOT Centre during its development. Its purpose was to be a blueprint of what is to come and stimulate park goers to develop new ideas that would propel humankind into the future. Many of the rides at EPCOT were aspirational in nature, yet utterly inspiring.

I remember one ride was like a monorail tram that took us on a tour of various possibilities in our lifetime. It was a gentle journey through time that brilliantly showcased the potential capabilities of humankind. The narrative began with history and our past and ended with the future. The ride showcased possibilities like the microwave oven, the wireless phone, a camera on a phone and what seemed like it could only be considered a flying car. There was also a sign at the end of that ride that read: IF YOU CAN DREAM IT, YOU CAN BUILD IT. My 5-year-old mind was in awe. At the time, I did not completely understand what the sign meant, but it shifted something in me. I thought, could I really build anything that I think of in this world? How was that possible?

After we exited the ride, I talked to my grandmother about my musings. My grandmother, who never failed to feed my curiosity and expand my little mind, listened to me attentively and patiently. She was a woman who understood the importance of exploration and helped me bridge the gap between what I knew and what I did not know as best she could. I asked her what was meant by the sign at the end of the ride. I remember her telling me that "the human brain is a powerful thing. We have the ability to figure out the solution to any problem if we take our time and think it all the way through."

She explained that, when she was a little girl, humans had just invented cars. Meanwhile, the ride we had just exited had flying cars. She told me that the animated sitcom The Jetsons, an interpretation of life in the 21st century, provided a comical view into what would become the reality in my lifetime. She then made a very definitive statement and told me, "And you, Ericka, will be a part of the future." I was amazed at the idea that I was going to be a part of the future. I was going to be a part of creating change in the world. This made me so excited and, it was at that point that I wanted to help change the world for the better. How could I help build the flying cars of the future? What did I need to do? How could I start? While at that moment I could not fully understand the intricacies of what my grandmother said. It was one of my earliest exposures to ambition, motivation, and achievement. I understood at that moment that it did not matter who I was or what I had. All that mattered was that I knew I was a part of the future. I was inspired to dream, and I knew I could build that dream if I wanted to.

My experience at the EPCOT Centre was significant for me. It was my aha moment. I remember it like it happened yesterday because it planted the seeds of excitement and optimism within me. Since childhood, I have been extremely optimistic about all of what was to come in my life. I have never been sure about what my future would look like, but I have always been certain that everything would turn out well no matter what happened. I had always been encouraged, from a young age, to do my best. I did not receive a blueprint of what the results would be, but I was often reminded that if I did my best, and used the tools at my disposal, everything would turn out well.

You may or may not have visited Disney's EPCOT Centre, but if you think back on your life, you will remember your own big and small awestruck moments. Perhaps it came to you in the form of a Disney Princess. In the Disney film, The Little Mermaid, Ariel was a mermaid princess who would dream of living on land as a human being — a wish that no others in the ocean dared to pursue. That did not stop Ariel, who successfully pursued her dream with complete optimism and hope. As she sang in the song "Daring to Dance," Who says that my dreams have to stay just my dreams, Ariel turned her dream into her reality. How did you feel when you watched James Cameron's blockbuster film Avatar revolutionize 3-D films? Perhaps it was Buzz Lightyear's classic trademark phrase, "To infinity… and beyond," from the film Toy Story. Did that phrase spark the feeling of optimism and limitless potential within you? Were you a fan of the game show Who Wants to Be a Millionaire? where host Regis Philbin planted the possibility that the average person could become a millionaire?

Growing up, I mostly saw poverty around me. There were many families in the neighborhood who were struggling to afford necessities and make ends meet to pay their bills. Despite what I saw around me, I was optimistic and hopeful that I would grow up and live a different lifestyle. What happened in your past, or what is happening in your life now, does not dictate what is next for you. Life is truly what you make of it and what you create for yourself. I did not believe that the lifestyle that I had growing up, in the neighborhood I grew up in, was going to be the rest of my life. I did not know what my future looked like, but I knew it was going to be very different from the one I had growing up. For you to achieve your greatest potential, you must be willing to dream up BIG AUDACIOUS GOALS (B.A.G.) with awe and optimism, see beyond uncertainties, and ultimately have unwavering faith in yourself.

If you believe in a higher power, whether it is God, the universe, energy, or something else, you will be a vessel of that higher power. You were chosen to be on this earth by a divine force and, as a representation of that higher power, you must trust that you have an important purpose to fulfill. Your purpose is limitless. To develop faith in yourself, to achieve your greatest potential, you must begin with self-acceptance and self-worth. Believe and know that you are valuable and that will create the necessary optimism and hope that you need within you to reach your highest potential. Believing in yourself takes work. If you are anything like young Ericka Pittman, then you are likely your own biggest enemy.

In spite of all the foundational work my family did to build me up, I stood in my own way for much of my life, especially during my younger years. Growing up I was not competitive. I did not want to try anything new or put myself in a situation where I could potentially fail. In other words, I had such little faith in myself that I essentially became my own barrier to reaching my highest potential. My extraordinary mother placed so many opportunities in front of me and encouraged me to try my hand at them. She wanted to offer me as many experiences as possible to explore what was out in the world for me. I remember consistently saying "Mom I don't have a talent. I wasn't born with one." She used to say the only way you can figure out what you are good at is by trying something new. Each time that she pushed me to try a new challenge or experience, like tennis or the school spelling bee competition, I would simply refuse.

I was afraid of falling short and I was a sore loser who did not want to fail. I never told her why I didn't want to do the things she was offering. I just brushed them off citing my "lack of interest" in the activities. If you are anything like young Ericka Pittman then you may remember a time or two where you've let yourself down and cheated yourself out of your goals, your purpose, and your greatest potential because you were afraid to fail. I spent many of my childhood and youth years convincing myself that it would be easier and better for me to not run the risk of failure. I thought it was easier not to compete and see just how far my potential could take me than to deal with being mad at myself for not coming out on top.

My childhood and youth taught me that the real loser was the one who sat on the sidelines. I discovered that, each time that I watched my peers compete. Sometimes they won and sometimes they lost, but they always seemed to come out fulfilled. I was doing myself the greatest disservice of all. My fear of failure robbed me of my motivation and had me playing a small game in life. Fortunately, this lack of desire to compete with others and the fear of failure did not show up in my professional life likely because my career did not feel like a competition with others. The only person I was up against was myself. I knew what my goals were, and I clearly saw the vision that I had for me. While I am not one to compete with the outside world, I have always held very high standards for myself.

Perhaps somewhat improbably, I had never been afraid to embark on a new career path. I had always been unapologetic about moving forward onto the next phase in my career. I learned to see my career as a competition with myself and not anyone else. I saw my career as a personal journey and there was a bigger stake on the line for me — this was the motivation that I needed to push myself. What was at stake for me, when it came to my career, was financial security. Growing up I saw, first-hand, and the impact of not having money. Financial security for me meant more than just paying the bills. It meant having independence, having the ability to make choices, and having the peace of mind that things would be financially taken care of.

I was motivated to have the things that financial security would give me, and I wanted the same for my family.

I watched my mother, grandmother and aunt work so hard and I wanted to create a life for them where they would not have to work as hard as they did before. Pushing myself to my greatest potential in my career meant that I would have expanded experiences, opportunities for promotion, ultimately achieving greater income and having endless earning potential. To this day, I am still motivated by security, or in other words, money. Having the means to make decisions, rather than just for basic survival needs like food and shelter, is important to me. It is equally important to me that my immediate family members also have the same financial flexibility and independence.

I am also just as motivated to create a life of financial independence for my future children so that they always feel secure and free to make life decisions independent of money. Being a woman in her 40s, I have entered my highest earning years as most people's highest earning potential is between 40 to 50 years of age. While some professionals in their 40s are focused on and are planning for their retirement, that is not the case for me. As a woman in her 40s who plans to have her own family one day, I have to think about my future child. I now think about my life in the context of being an aging or older parent. For the next 20 years, I would be close to or in retirement, but I will still have to put a child through college which will likely be much costlier in 20 years. This is a lot of pressure for me and I feed off that pressure. It motivates me to work as smart as I can, create the highest earning potential opportunities for myself in my career and achieve the best financial outcomes that I possibly can. I am building for myself and my current and future family — just as my mother, aunt, and grandmother before them, did.

Shortly after returning from our family trip to Disney World, I began to muse about EPCOT Centre and the idea that "If you can dream it, you can build it." I started to ask my grandmother about all the different things I could do in life. I didn't label it or recognize it as such at that time, but I was exploring my options. My grandmother and I played a game that we liked to call, "What can I be when I grow up?" No matter what I asked, my grandmother's responses were always the same, "anything you want," "of course," "yes" she would say.

"Can I be a firefighter?" I would ask.

"Yes."

"Can I be a police officer?"

"Of course."

"Can I be a nurse, a doctor, lawyer, and an astronaut?"

"You can be anything you want Ericka. Just put your mind to it and you can achieve all your dreams."

My grandmother matched my optimism and hope with every answer she gave. Until, years later, I asked her, "Nana, can I be the president of the United States?" At that moment, my grandmother paused and turned to look at me. For the first time, she gave an answer that I had never heard from her before. She said, "Someday sunshine… someday." As a woman who had lived through the assassination of Dr. Martin Luther King Jr. and the civil rights movement, she knew that I was still a black woman living in a society that did not treat me equally.

What my grandmother wanted me to understand on my own was that, despite the human spirit and my abundant potential, I would have to work hard to break barriers and overcome obstacles. My grandmother cautioned that the world can be a cold, lonely, and uncompromising place that wouldn't see me as an equal for several reasons. None of these reasons would be any fault of my own but they would pose obstacles in my ability to truly have any option available to me. While I did not become the president of the United States, I am proud to say that a black man became a U.S. president in my lifetime. He worked hard and earned his place in the White House and many of us not only got to witness that historic moment but were also a part of it. His rise to success makes it that much easier for me to answer, "YES YOU CAN" when my future daughter asks me if she can become the president of the United States of America. That is why, like thousands of other Americans, I volunteered for Barack Obama's 2008 presidential campaign.

Even though I lived in New Jersey at the time, I would drive to Philadelphia (which is in the swing state of Pennsylvania) to canvass for the Obama campaign. I walked through many neighborhoods, up and down people's driveways, and knocked on doors to encourage people to vote. I registered people to vote in real-time so that they could go down to the polls and make their voices heard. During this experience, I remembered that conversation with my grandmother from my childhood and I knew that I was contributing to the future. I was a part of creating the change that the world needed. I knew that years from that moment, a young black girl could consider becoming the president of the United States of America and it would not be an impossible notion. That option would be available to her because thousands of us were on the ground working to break that barrier by helping to elect America's first black president. My experience volunteering on the Obama campaign brought me to tears and made me feel so fulfilled to give back to my community in such a significant way.

While becoming the nation's president was not, and likely will not be, in my cards, I have made progress and achieved my own important milestones. Throughout my career, there have been people who second-guessed my ability to make executive decisions or be a strong leader. I encountered many skeptics when I was younger and just starting out in the corporate world, and I continue to experience that. Some people questioned my potential and my leadership because I was a woman, others because I was young, and now still appearing young, and others because I was a person of color. I am aware of all the barriers and the stereotypes that are tied to me as I go through my life and career striving to impact the world and create change. Despite the obstacles, I continue to believe that "If you can dream it, you can build it."

For me, this phrase means that anything is possible.

Anyone can have the life they desire, and anyone can impact the world in significant ways. Where you start your story and the resources you have at hand don't matter because what is most important is how resourceful you are with the tools you have been given in life. For anyone with an idea or dream, I am here to tell you that you can achieve it. Before humans were able to put a man on the moon, the notion of ascending to space was just an idea. It started off as a dream but now that is our reality. Human beings have solved the puzzle of how to successfully travel into space and to the moon. What is important is that you follow your dreams with massive amounts of action. The dream is only the seed that is the beginning of turning possibility into reality.

It was only when I started to live with the mind-set of abundance that I stepped out of my comfort zone and fears to try my hand at a bigger game in life and have the life that I desired. Having it all means different things to different people. Don't let others dictate what your definition of having "it all" means to you and don't be ashamed of what you want for your life. Pursue your ideas and dreams with fervor and don't be afraid to fail. Try, fail, try again, fail again, and try some more. It is the only way to win at life and be on a constant journey of learning and discovery. While I avoided failure as a young person, I now embrace it and have experienced my fair share of failures.

I had always wanted to be a real estate mogul. I grew up in a "renter family" and had only been a renter for many years. No one in my immediate lineage had ever owned property before. I wanted to be an owner and had dreams of becoming a landlord. As a young adult in the early years of my career, I decided to pursue this dream and become a real estate investor, acquiring properties with the intention of renting them to generate profit. At the time, there was a housing bubble and the no-doc loan mortgage structure was the hottest trend in the real estate market. No-doc loan mortgages allowed borrowers to obtain funds from lenders with very little documentation. In other words, borrowing funds became more accessible. A mortgage specialist advised me that it would be easier for me to secure funding from lenders if I purchased two to three homes together at once as opposed to borrowing for one at a time. Uncharacteristic of me at the time, I decided to take a leap and jump into the real estate market to pursue my dream of becoming an investor and real estate mogul.

Before I knew it, I had purchased five properties and was leasing them out. I thought I had tried and figured it all out. I would purchase homes two to three at a time, renovate them, rent them out, and then ultimately flip them to increase my overall net worth. What I did not factor in my master plan was all the things that could go wrong when managing rental properties, including issues with the tenants, wear and tear on the property, and missed rental payments. Let us not begin to discuss the housing bubble of '07. While my net worth had increased significantly and quickly, so had my stress level and the issues I had to manage. The whole experience was like a bad nightmare. In the end, four years later, I decided that I no longer wanted to be a real estate mogul/investor. The experience was one that helped me learn and grow, among other benefits. I used the equity from a couple of the properties to buy my perfect primary dwelling to live in myself. Fortunately for me, I was able to leverage the opportunity to make lemonade out of, what felt like, sheer rotten lemons. I learned the nuances of real estate investing, and I learned a lot about myself by pursuing this dream and essentially failing at it. I also learned what I can achieve when I prioritize my ideas and dreams.

Throughout my life, the kind of woman that I needed to be, to achieve the things that I did, is someone quite selfish. I had to prioritize myself.. In making myself number one, everything else became secondary and everything else had to fit around my dreams and desires. We live in a society where people, especially women, are made to feel that being selfish is negative, but it is not. Being selfish is important and it is necessary to achieve your dreams. As women, we tend to put ourselves on the back burner too often.

So many women make their ambitions priority number two. Your dreams are your own and only you can make them your reality. We often create obstacles for ourselves, knowing or unknowingly. The stories we tell ourselves to validate the status quo, live as society tells us to, and be what others expect us to be will often squander our goals and limit our potential. What has worked tremendously well for me is to know that my purpose and the work that I do are very important. What has also proven dividends for me is to unapologetically be myself and embrace the authentic version of me.

Someone I admire for transforming her life and achieving her dreams, by being her authentic self, is American rapper

Cardi B. She has opened my eyes to the power of vulnerability and being true to who you are. She is living her best life by being herself and the world completely accepts and loves her for it. Cardi B is being exactly who a higher power has created her to be. In a world where so many people follow the line, she has embraced her story, one that is full of moments where she is going against the norm and straying from what society deems to be acceptable or appropriate. If Cardi B allowed the opinions of society to determine her potential or decide what she could or could not achieve, she would not have become a wife, a mother, or the first solo female rapper since Lauryn Hill in 1998 to hit number one on the Billboard Hot 100 and the 2017 hip-hop anthem of the summer. With her song "Bodak Yellow," and her unapologetic lyrics like the line "Look, I don't dance now, I make money moves," she references her former life as an exotic dancer in a strip club. She does not hide even the part of her life that is shamed in our world where patriarchy and misogyny still exist. She is proud of all parts of herself. She has mastered the art of using vulnerability and authenticity to her advantage.

One of my favorite quotes, from a poem by Robert Browning, is "Ah, but a man's reach should exceed his grasp, or what's a heaven for?" I love this quote because it is a call to attempt the impossible and just go for it. If you do not stretch yourself, you will never know the depth and extent of your possibilities. You must reach far beyond what you believe is within your grasp. Your ambition must surmount what you believe you are capable of, as that is the way to achieve your infinite potential.

Sean Combs, musician and entrepreneur extraordinaire, inspires me tremendously in his ambitions. He does not take no for an answer in the pursuit of his ambitions. He has both reasonable and unreasonable goals — both of which he pursues in the most quintessential manner. Having had the privilege of working with him closely, it is almost unreal to watch him. I have been inspired by his vision for the future, but even more inspired by how firm he is on achieving it.

The reality is that being unreasonable creates innovation and change in the world. If the Wright brothers, Orville and Wilbur, had been convinced that a piece of metal could not fly in the sky, then we would not have airplanes. Electricity was unreasonable before it became the norm, the light bulb was unreasonable at one time, and the thought of communicating without having to personally deliver the message was once considered impossible. It is important to have a level of unreasonableness and childlike wonder in your ambitions to reach your infinite potential.

AMBITION

When I was young, my mother always used to tell me to pay careful attention to my first mind. "Your first mind is your instinct," she would say, adding that I should allow it to be my guiding compass, regardless of how certain or uncertain I felt about what my instinct was telling me to do. Trusting your gut feeling is a learned process and it takes practice to master. By going through my own process of learning to trust my instincts, I have been able to embrace uncertainty and take the kinds of chances that I otherwise would not have. Many people do not trust their instinct or embrace uncertainty because they are operating out of fear.

One of the primary blocks that prevent humans from greatness is FEAR. Some people are afraid to fail, while others are afraid that they might be great. Fear is what causes us to view uncertainty negatively and as something that could harm us when that is far from the truth. What if American athlete Michael Phelps let his fear of greatness get the best of him? The world would not have witnessed one of the greatest displays of athleticism and achievement in aquatics in 2008 when Phelps won eight gold medals at the Beijing Summer Olympics. What if the, black anti-apartheid activist, who entered prison on Robben Island in 1964, was seized and stopped in action by the uncertainty ahead of him? Thirty years later, humanity would not have seen or felt the impact of Nelson Mandela — one of history's greatest freedom fighters — and he would not have been elected as South Africa's first black president. These individuals, along with others, have inspired many actions in my own life.

Moving to and living in Los Angeles for the last few years has been one of my biggest adventures. Prior to making my big move, I had never lived outside of New York and I had not been a six-hour plane ride away from my family. Along with my geographical move, I also took a chance professionally and moved to a new role within Combs Enterprises. I became the chief marketing officer at AQUAhydrate Inc. Even though I knew that this was a high-turnover executive position — most chief marketing officers have an average tenure of 18-24 months in that role with an organization — I still took a chance. This was an opportunity for me to provide marketing and strategic leadership for a company that was still in a late-stage start-up phase, which presented its own uncertainties. I was leaving behind my prominent role in New York to take on a position that I knew could very likely be my last stop at Combs Enterprises, a company that I had served for almost a decade. I decided to take the leap and deviate from the plan while replaying the words of Jay-Z, "Son said Hov, how you get so fly? I said, from not being afraid to fall out the sky."

Along with embracing uncertainty in my professional life, I also took a chance in my personal life. I decided to embark on a romantic relationship and be very vulnerable with a significant other. Vulnerability to me means to fully accept yourself and come to terms with all your experiences without judgment. I took a chance and was open about my feelings and I started from a place of trust from the beginning. This was difficult for me at first because I was putting myself out there for assessment, opinions, and possible ridicule. While that relationship ended in extreme betrayal and heartbreak, it was a valuable life lesson for me. Allowing myself to give, gave me comfort in knowing who I am, what I want and what works in my life. It has also taken some of the sting out of the expectations around relationships. The regret of never trying is far greater for me than the risk of disappointment.

> **"The regret of never trying is far greater for me than the risk of disappointment.**

Think about your own life and consider the areas where you are holding back, you are being constrained by your own thoughts, and are being fearful of uncertainty. Are you afraid to make a career change and follow your passions? Is there fear about having a difficult conversation with a loved one that you have been putting off for a long time? Do you want to just leave it all to travel and experience the world? As you come across these moments in your life, get present to them and try to understand at a deeper level where the fear is coming from. You must think about and weigh the sacrifices you will have to make to fulfill your dreams, but do not let those sacrifices deter you from living life with childlike wonder. Take the chance, embrace uncertainty, and make a leap. If you fail, you will try again. There is no time in your life where you cannot reinvent yourself or dream another dream.

Facing your fears and living life in the way that only your first mind can guide you is an achievement on its own, regardless of the results. You must celebrate these small, and large, victories in your life. Being in a state of gratitude and self-recognition will allow you to appreciate these moments. Facing your fears and embracing uncertainty is no small feat and celebrating it will reinforce just how far you have come and just how far you have the potential to go.

AMBITION, MOTIVATION, AND ACHIEVEMENT

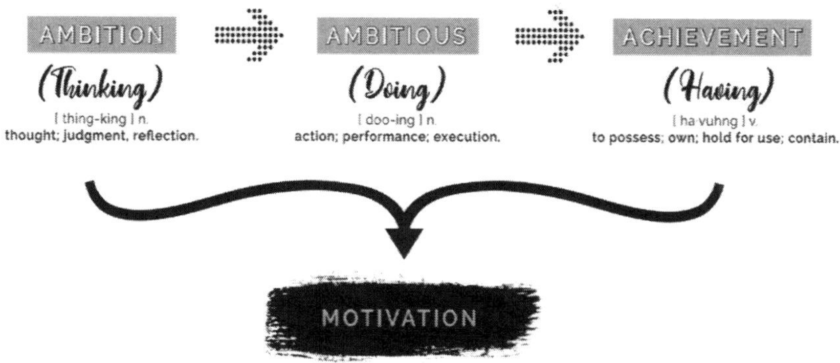

Each of us has the same 24 hours in a day. In other words, we have 1,440 minutes that we are granted and can use to make something amazing happen. With the time that we are given, we can choose to focus our energy on building a flourishing future or we can allow our future to happen to us. Neither is right or wrong, but they are both a choice. I choose to do what is necessary to build the best future for myself, knowing that it will require an investment of time, actions, and energy. The sobering reality is, we have little time to live on this Earth. At best, we have maybe 80 good years. If you are lucky enough to make it to 100, then good for you, but there is only so much you can do between 80 and 100 years of age. This is a "use it or lose it" game we are playing. There are no dress rehearsals. Honestly, 80 years is not a tremendous amount of time at all, yet it is plenty of time for everything we want in life.

To build the best future for yourself and find success,

there are three critical elements for you to be mindful of.

1. Ambition

2. Motivation

3. Achievement

While these three elements may seem obvious and simple, they are often reduced from their greatness to mere doubt, negativity, and fear. We can often become a hindrance to ourselves and become our greatest enemy.

AMBITION

Ambition is the unrelenting desire and internal conviction to accomplish an objective. It is the reason you begin to do the necessary work required in the first place. Everyone possesses some level of ambition, but not everyone is ambitious. Those who are ambitious back their desires with a lot of action. Ambition requires care, nurturing, and monitoring to be sustained over time. It is not easy to maintain your ambition for the long haul and to do so requires active management. I sustain my own ambitions by reviewing and renewing my commitment to my desires and required action regularly, often daily. We are all human and we are all guilty of losing our way sometimes when it comes to ambition. Life has a way of distracting us from the things that are most important to us. The GREAT news is each day is a new opportunity to RENEW our commitments and realign with what is most important. I have days when I don't operate at 200 percent, or even 50 percent sometimes, but I find a way to be gentle with myself. I address the underlying issues that prevented me from acting and I hit reset and get focused. Each day I think about my goals and re-pledge my promise to fulfill on them.

Active management of my ambitions also includes close monitoring of the things that could stand in my way of fulfilling them. I remain present to the pitfalls that I often fall prey to and catch myself each time that I am impacted by them again. It is important to think about and be aware of all the things that talk you out of your ambitions — the people, the excuses, and the self-defeating thoughts. I encourage you to write a list of all the things that stand in your way of being ambitious. Refer to this list regularly. After reading each statement, ask yourself... Is this statement true? More times than not the stories we make up in our head are just that, STORIES they are not fact based and rarely have merit. This exercise is a helpful tool to keep yourself in check and differentiate when your reason for not acting is legitimate and when it is not. My own list consists of time constraints, exhaustion, self-doubt, and overanalysis.

Having ambition, but not acting, will not help you reach your greatest potential. It is like life. Just because I am breathing does not mean I am living. Breathing does mean that I am alive, but that alone is not enough to be truly living my best life. As you think about your ambitions, also think about the actions you have taken and the actions that you will take to realize them. Some people start off with ambition but do not shift to ambitious mode. Shifting from thinking to doing requires motivation.

MOTIVATION

Motivation is the reason why we do what we do. It is your "why." It's the feeling that is driven by your "why." Discovering and becoming present to your "why" is what it takes to shift from ambition to ambitious, from thinking to doing. You will know when you have found your motivation when it causes you to exercise self-control and discipline that will ultimately allow you to act on your aspirations. Motivation is the inspiration that guides and fuels your ambitions. It sustains the actions needed to achieve your goals. Motivation is not a constant and it will not last unless it is nurtured regularly. Rekindling your motivation, especially after a failure or setback, is a necessary part of the process. Motivation is like your energy, it can be refueled even after it is drained. Motivation is also fleeting, and it is discipline and consistency that will keep you on track to meet your goals.

Constantly being mindful of your "why" will help you increase your motivation. If saving money to buy a home for your family to grow is more important than a summer vacation, then you will find the motivation and discipline to forgo the trip and save for your new home. If your "why" statement is not strong or is not inspiring, then you are more likely to be persuaded to go on the trip. Once you are clear on your "why" statement, write it down and place it where it will be visible to you. There is power in writing down your thoughts. I encourage you to write down three reasons why you want to achieve a certain objective or dream. Your reasons should be based on the root of your inspiration. Internalize these reasons and regularly remind yourself of them. The simpler your "why" statements are, the more powerful and impactful they will be. My general rule is to keep it simple because when things get complex, you are more likely to lose focus and get overwhelmed.

What is your goal?

____

____

____

____

Why do you want to achieve your goal?

____

____

____

____

Once you have your "why" statements, I encourage you to share them with other trusted sources. I believe it is healthy to communicate your motivations in your personal life and your professional life. Throughout my career, I have always been vocal about the fact that money is an important motivator for me. I have always wanted my bosses to know that I prefer monetary compensation over public recognition, accolades, or power. Communicating this has allowed me to be recognized in the way that I want to be received and bring out my greatest potential. An ex-boyfriend of mine worked in sales and was driven by his desire to be the top sales performer. He often received awards for his work with the company with which he was employed, and he would display them proudly. The accolades were so important to him. Meanwhile, my thought process was, "who cares about the awards, where is your bonus"' And "how will this impact your promotion?" He had no desire to aim for a promotion or a raise. His goal was to do a great job in his role and the accolades were proof of his efforts. Each of us have different motivations and you cannot assume that other people will know what motivates you. Be clear and honest with yourself about what you want, and do not be afraid to communicate it to others.

ACHIEVEMENT

Achievement comes when ambition plus ambitiousness meets motivation. It is the result that stems from the fruit of your labor. Achievement is the fulfillment of successfully accomplishing your vision, objective, and what you set out to do. My ambition was to write a book, my motivation was to help other women by sharing my knowledge and lessons with them, and my achievement is my completed and published book. Achievement is the magical transition of literally turning nothing into something. It is no small feat and must be celebrated.

It is vital to celebrate your achievements. From the time we are born, we learn about praise and celebration. Our parents cheer us on when we first learn to crawl, we get recorded when we take our first step, and our smallest victories as a child are praised. As we get older, though, there is a shift that occurs.

Our achievements are taken for granted, we are not often in the spotlight, and the responsibility to celebrate falls on our own shoulders, for the most part. While it is more natural for adults to be harsh on ourselves when we fail, we are less likely to take the time to revel in our successes. By shifting our mind-set and training ourselves to be kinder and gentler to our process, we will more often shift to a positive state of mind and be more inspired. Celebrating your achievements does not have to take up a lot of time, energy, or money. Sometimes I will celebrate by going on vacation and other times it is the simpler things, like buying myself flowers or taking a bath in the soaker tub with candles lit, both equally important and impactful.

I like to visualize my achievements. I have a goal chart on which I post stickers for every win I achieve. I do this for my small victories and the big ones. I use these stickers to see how close I am to achieving the bigger ambition. Going through the process of completing my book, I give myself a gold star for each chapter that I complete. As I write these words, I am on chapter 4 and I am excited to give myself a sticker at the end of this chapter. I also love mantras and I like to speak kind and encouraging words to myself. Saying things like "You got this, Ericka," "Yes, Ericka, you did it momma," and "Way to go, girl". These are just a few of the ways I celebrate my achievements.

CREATE AND EMBRACE YOUR FUTURE

I am always visualizing. I use visuals to not only cele-brate my achievements and monitor my progress, but also to create my future. I recently worked on my vision board. I pulled out some magazines and left myself free to cut out clippings of images and words that resonated with me. Once I had glued all my clippings and completed my vision board, I was amazed at all that was within my heart. My board was all about strength, resilience, an evolution. It was a display of a new Ericka Pitt-man, a new future, and focused on manifesting the greatness within me. It made me realize just how much of my potential has not been realized and I was ready to embrace it.

Preparing for my future includes being aware and in the N.O.W. with my present self. I meditate daily to identify deep-er with my purpose and infinite potential. Understanding what I have been put on this Earth to do, and how I can fulfill it, for me is ultimately about listening for God and being ready when God speaks to me. This is a constant work in progress and learning process for me. I have yet to master being and living completely in the present while manifesting the future. As I work toward the achievement of my goals and dreams, I am aware that once I achieve a goal or dream, it will then become a part of my past. The future is exciting, but it will be fleeting to solely focus on it. Missing out on the present will mean that I will experience short moments of the future which will quickly become a part of my past.

In creating your future, be open to new possibilities and

be flexible on how you can get there. Always remember: Having things work out is far more important than HOW things work out. When it was time for me to go to college, I imagined a future where I would be living on my own and attending college outside of New York. I resisted the fact that I stayed in New York and attended a local college. However, in hindsight, studying at City University of New York-Baruch College proved to be very beneficial for me and helped me create a future that I could not have imagined. While I would not have known in the present, at the time, that I was making the decision, it ended up being the best path forward for my future. Create your future but be open to the many ways that you can achieve it. There is no straightforward path into the future and you must examine your past to recognize that.

I not only love creating a vision for my future, but I also enjoy looking back to the past and seeing the vision that I had created for myself before. I regularly revisit my previous vision boards and see what I have accomplished and reflect on how I have evolved as a person. Journaling is also a powerful tool to help you through your evolution of self and manifestation of the future. I have multiple journals that I use simultaneously, each serving a unique purpose. I have a gratitude journal that I write in daily to remind myself of all the things for which I must be thankful. In my dream journal, I write the details each time I have profound dreams to help me reflect on what is on my subconscious mind. Then there is my regular musings and emotions journal that I turn to when I am inspired to jot down my ideas, thoughts, and feelings at that moment.

I purchase a new regular journal for myself every 10 years, whether I have used all the pages of the existing journal or not. For me, every decade of my life is a new chapter. I am always inspired to go back and read each chapter of my life because it is a display of my growth and change. It makes up the various narratives that have created who I am today. I love to go back and laugh at myself and reflect on the times that I took things way too seriously. Life has a way of working itself out for the highest good. I don't always have to DO anything to have it work out. I can simply BE my best self, accept things for what they are, and move in the path of least resistance to have the most ideal outcome.

The human spirit is a miraculous and resilient thing. As we go through life, somewhere along the way, we tend to lose sight of our greatness and lose touch with our childlike wonder. It is important to constantly remind yourself that you can be anything you want to be, so think about who you want to be in this world. Before you can fulfill your purpose, it is necessary to get clear on the future that you want to manifest. Get even clearer on the WHY behind who you want to be. Connect your vision with daily practices that will help you achieve the future you are creating. Create the life you want to live with childlike wonder and embrace it with your heart and soul.

PITTMAN'S RULES:

1. "If You Can Dream It, You Can Build It."
2. Be selfish and prioritize yourself.
3. Unapologetically be your authentic self.
4. Actively manage your ambitions.
5. Discover your "why" and keep it simple.
6. Celebrate your own achievements.
7. Approach your future with childlike wonder and embrace it.
8. You don't always have to DO anything to have it work out. You can simply BE your best self to have the most ideal outcome.

GET AHEAD OF THE GAME

Society, cultural norms, technology, the world of business and just about everything else in life is changing at a rapid pace. To keep up with the change, you must stay in the game and be aware of what is altering around you. To achieve extraordinary success though, you must anticipate what is not yet in existence. As you move through the various phases of your life — high school, college, your first job, progressive roles in your career, and career transitions — you must think about what will make you stand out from the pack. Ask yourself the question, what can I do now that will put me ahead in the future?

The most obvious area of rapid change in our world is in technology. In my lifetime, we went from not knowing what the Internet was ('Wait, so what is that exactly?')to dial-up Internet access on our desktops to now being virtually connected to just about anything. We have smart TVs, the Apple watch, and even our lamps at home are "smart" (think Alexa and Google Home). It is important to be present and aware of the cadence of change because we must adjust as the world around us shifts. If you do not keep up, you will very quickly become irrelevant and be left behind. As a woman in her 40s, I am aware that I live in a world where there is a generation that does not know what a fax machine or a typewriter is, or rather WAS. I know that a handwritten letter no longer holds the same value that it used to because this is the era of social media communication. Even grammar rules have changed — you no longer need to use the double-space rule after punctuated sentences. People are now using acronyms like GM (Goodmorning) and THX (Thanks) on professional email correspondence, GIFs, videos, pictures, hashtags, and emoji to communicate. Technology has also shifted the pace of business. It is truly a different world.

With the increased capability for a shorter turn-around time, we are expected to make decisions and complete work faster. We used to have more time to process information, both emotionally and pragmatically. That is no longer the case. With the invention of laptops, mobile devices and in-flight Wi-Fi access, flying on a business trip no longer means six hours of quiet time. I am literally editing this chapter in-flight as I fly back to Los Angeles from a board meeting in North Carolina. In the past, it could take a week for two parties, if it had to be mailed to one another, to sign a document through postal service. Today, we can sign documents on our smartphones. With the modern luxuries of technology, we now must get accustomed to processing information in shorter periods of time, make decisions faster, and getting more work done in smaller increments of time. Even if it is not possible to keep pace with the rapid change of technology, we must at least keep up and never stay more than a few steps behind.

If we don't recognize the volatility of the changes around us, we will quickly succumb to them. Thus, it is essential for us to master our ability to understand change and quickly apply it to our own lives and the way we work. Resisting the shifts in the world will only cost you in the long run. Change is a constant and we must embrace it to succeed. Having said that, it is okay to remove yourself from the constant buzz around you occasionally. We all need a break. Taking short stints of time away from social media or your smartphone is necessary, and it is healthy in the quest for balance. It will allow you to recharge and come back to take on the busy world we live in.

Succeeding in a constantly evolving world requires that you identify and be aware of the change, accept it, and embrace it. Sometimes we can get so caught up in the routine and business of our lives that we don't even realize the shifts that are occurring around us. When a change feels sudden or abrupt then it will likely make you feel unprepared for it. The reality is abrupt, and sudden changes are a course correction in your life. When things change rapidly, and often without notice, it usually is a precursor to an amazing shift that is to come for you. The key is to go with the flow and take the path of least resistance. Just ride the wave and dial into your present self.

There will always be shifts in the world around you and in your life that will be a surprise, however, in most cases, there will always be signs. We are either not in tune with the present enough to see what's up ahead or we choose to ignore the signs that they are coming. While the change can be scary, it is a constant in life and therefore, we must accept it. If something isn't evolving, then it likely means that it is dead. Therein lies the reason for the season of change. There is value in the rebirth of the Earth during spring. Even Mother Nature shows us how natural and necessary change is. Your life is no different. You should be changing, you should be adapting, and you should be using moments of change as opportunities for the rebirth of the improved and evolved version of you.

At its core, accepting change is knowing that it will happen and being okay with it. Embracing change, on the other hand, is looking forward to it from a positive space and being grateful for it. There is a tremendous amount of unknowing in change. You don't always know what is next. Trusting in the natural order of things requires a faith that you already have, just look at your life. Every single part of your life is an example of change gone right because you are still here. You are reading this book. You are looking for ways to grow and be a better human. That tells me that, no matter your circumstances, you use shifts in your life to grow.

I am currently going through a major change in my life right now. I have parted ways with Combs Enterprises, an organization that I successfully contributed to and had grown with for the past nine years. The change was sudden, but I knew it was coming. I saw the signs leading up to the departure and I had been, slowly but surely, simultaneously working to get ahead of it. I made the focus of 2018 my own brand. I have been thinking about my personal social media strategy, my first book, and making the right connections to take me to the next phase of my career. The most uncomfortable part of this life transition for me is that, for the first time, I am dealing with a change and I don't have a master plan for it. I am not sure what is next for me and, oddly, I like it. While I don't know what my next steps are, I have never been surer in my life that what's next is so right and amazing for me! I am open and ready for the path of least resistance. Whatever is next, I'm here for it and I know it is going to turn out great because it always has.

To be clear, moving away from Combs Enterprises

hasn't been easy. I have had my fair share of moments of anxiety and nervousness. Along with making decisions about my next career move, I also must make serious personal decisions about whether I am going to continue to live in Los Angeles where I have built a life for myself or move back to New York full time and be closer to family and warm network. In the past, this type of transition would have made me insane. It would have made me unsettled, and emotional about how my life was playing out. It would have made me lose confidence in myself and I would have struggled to get back on track. Today, as the person that I have evolved to be, I am open to the possibilities of what is to come next for me. I am excited about the uncertainty, the opportunity and freedom to be and do something different in my life. I am embracing this change as a welcomed break from what became my norm.

I was exhausted, and I felt like a hamster stuck on a wheel with no end in sight. I was the textbook definition of burned out. I have been at this hustle, this grind, for 23 years straight. I knew I wanted something different for my life, but I did not have the time nor the energy to fully explore what that could look like while juggling an extremely demanding job. I see this transition in my life as a sign from the universe that my time in this space was up. I am using this new season in my life as an opportunity to move on to something new and different. As of now, I am still exploring what that new and different something is. I am taking my time and enjoying this period of discovery and recharge. I am in no rush. Friends and family have asked me if I am afraid of being in this period of transition not knowing what is next for me. My answer has consistently been "not at all." In fact, I am excited. I have been preparing for this and that preparation makes me that much more confident in my ability to get the work done. Always be prepared in life and you will never be shocked by the change. Surprised, maybe, but shocked, no.

When it comes to change, time is of the essence. Embracing the shifts around you quickly and in a timely manner is the best way to capitalize on it. Don't allow yourself to be stopped by resistance or regret. Instead, focus on processing the change, the lesson there is in the situation for you to learn, and apply that knowledge to your life. I recently heard someone say "Fail Fast." I thought that was the most brilliant mantra. Failure is inevitable, we are all going to encounter it at some point or another in our life journey but get on with it, and quickly absorbing the lessons is the quickest route to achieve your next win. I used to suffer from what I like to refer to as the "should have, could have" syndrome. I often found myself obsessing over decisions that I have made, thinking about what could have happened if I'd made a different choice or responded to a situation in another way. Thinking about things that you cannot change is a waste of time. I am continuously learning to leave the past behind and focus on the present.

Being in the present is the only way to take advantage of the opportunities that change presents to you. Forgiveness is crucial to letting go of what cannot be undone. Forgive yourself and those around you for what has happened. Take the lesson in the experience and use it to become a better version of yourself. Focusing on the present with excitement and gratitude also makes the heartache of the past go away. If I obsessed over my departure from Combs Enterprises, then I would not have optimal mental and emotional capacity to work on my business plan. I arrived at that organization full and whole. I knew who I was. I knew what I could contribute and, regardless of how things turned out, good or bad, I knew who I was when I left. I was and always will be me so the experience had its moment in time and now I am moving on with my amazing life. Focusing on the "should have, could have" of a former relationship will not allow me to be in the now with a new experience. We will always have decisions to make and those decisions will always have an opportunity cost attached to them. It is also true that we will also have memories and they should simply live in the library of our minds as lessons learned and experiences had. Get complete with the decisions you have made in the past and leave them right there. You are now in the present and that is where your new life will happen. The sooner you get complete with the past, the faster you will get to contentment.

My life has been a series of dreams that I have identified and then I have reverse-engineered the steps to drive those dreams forward. Many of the steps I've taken have elevated me because they set me apart from the crowd. I learned to be comfortable with being uncomfortable. While I was in college studying Communications, I made the decision to work full-time during the day and go to school full-time in the evenings. I made this decision so that I could financially fund my education, but I found a way to elevate myself even in this decision. I identified an entry-level job in corporate communications that allowed me to not only fund my school tuition but also gain valuable work experience that put me ahead of my peers once I graduated from college. While everybody else graduated with a degree, I graduated with a degree and four years of relevant industry experience.

Even though I was young at the time that I attended college, I had the foresight to create a résumé that demonstrated both my theoretical background in Communications and real-world practical experience. It gave me a jump-start in my career that allowed me to accelerate ahead, especially in my 20s. To achieve extraordinary success, you must anticipate what is not yet in existence. The best piece of professional advice I have ever received is to take complete ownership of any role that you are in and treat it like it is your own business. Know that your contribution to the company is vital. Embody excellence as you do your current work knowing that it will lead to new work and new positions in the future, even roles that you may not have seen yourself in yet.

> **"Know that your contribution to the company is vital.**

I used to serve as the vice president of the chairman's office at Combs Enterprises, reporting directly to Sean Combs. Part of my role was to bridge the communication between the company's numerous portfolios; at the time there were nine businesses each having its own senior leader and the chairman. The other half of my role was to work on finding synergies across the various brands for efficiencies and greater impact. This opportunity was presented to me six years into being with the company. Not 90 days, not 18 months, but after six years of being an employee. Many people are looking for the microwave fix to their lives, but the reality is life is a HUGE oven-stuffer turkey that takes prepping, brining, marinating, and continuous basting for hours and hours (think years and years) to get it just right. And please believe that the bigger the turkey, the longer it takes to bake.

I spent six years being at Combs Enterprises being excellent in everything that I did. I checked all the boxes and did all that was required of my role, specifically for Sean Combs. Prior to being offered the new role, I had already worked on every single one of the company's portfolio brands in some capacity and had specific insight on each of the brands. I was able to capitalize on the opportunity when it came because I had been preparing for it for six years. Anticipating what is not yet in existence is about having a career plan and being ready.

The most fundamental ingredients of a strong career plan are flexibility and openness. I used to have a master plan for my personal life and my career. It was a detailed outline of exactly what I was going to do and the milestones I was going to reach with timelines next to each of them. When I was 16 years old, I thought I would be married to my high school sweetheart one year after I graduated from college, go to law school, and be full on into my career by the time I was 24. My plan was to be a wife, lawyer, and a mother all by 25 years old. What ended up happening was that my high school sweetheart cheated on me, got an underage girl in our neighborhood pregnant, and made me the laughingstock of our neighborhood in my sophomore year of college. My plan changed. I wasn't going to marry the boy I loved for four years, I no longer wanted to be a lawyer having realized my love for marketing, and well, plans are jokes for God's amusement. It was only when I changed the way I approached planning my life and career that I saw fundamental shifts. If you want radically different results in your life, you must make radically different decisions.

> "If you want radically different results in your life, **you must make radically different decisions.**

I finally realized that the detailed outline of my life that I created was the very thing that was stalling my progress. While I believe you should have goals and plans with tasks to achieve said goals, it is important to let your life flow. Timelines are effective for completing tasks to ensure that you are in action. Life, on the other hand, needs to be more flexible because it is impacted by variables that are outside your control. Variables such as other people, fluctuations in the economy, and changing life circumstances of dependents may require an alteration of your plans. Things are constantly changing in real life, so your plans need to be able to accommodate for these natural shifts.

Perfection is the enemy of done and, looking out for specific accomplishments, is the surest way to miss all your other achievements and growth that you did not plan out. I was missing the many blessings that the universe was sending my way because I was focused on fulfilling this intense master plan that I had. Modify the approach. Instead of an iron clad master plan, try to have a strategy. Having a strategy is like having a blueprint for your life and it is an effective tool to guide you. My current strategy is to develop and market my personal brand widely. My strategy to achieve this end goal is to publish my first book and have it on the shelves of bookstores across North America, go on a speaking tour across the country, secure a television deal, and launch my own line of lifestyle products. Having a blueprint provides me with goals to work toward and a timeline to target all while knowing that this is just a framework and not a master plan. I am flexible with my timelines and even my goals. I may secure a television deal before I go on a speaking tour or I may find another opportunity that completely replaces the initial goals that I had.

It is important to strike a healthy balance between being in the present and creating a blueprint for your future. To help me find this balance, I use the 3-6-9 strategy. This tool can be applied to hours, days, months, and years. Thus, it has the built-in flexibility of letting me focus on what's immediately ahead of me in the moment as well as my long-term vision. These are the questions I ask myself to use the 3-6-9 strategy:

What do I need to do in the next three, six, and nine hours to help me achieve my goals? How will this impact my life?

What do I need to do in the next three, six, and nine days to help me achieve my goals? How will this impact my life?

What do I need to do in the next three, six, and nine months to help me achieve my goals? How will this impact my life?

What do I need to do in the next three, six, and nine years to help me achieve my goals? How will this impact my life?

By mapping out how I will be spending my time in varied increments of time, I am able to make progress on my goals without feeling overwhelmed and while ensuring that it is contributing to my long-term vision. Breaking down your goals and dreams into smaller tasks, and tackling them bit by bit, will cause a compounding effect on the overall impact. The 3-6-9 strategy tool is effective in your personal life and in the workplace as well. It is a proven formula to help you maximize your time and energy by applying both strategically. Looking ahead into the long term will also help you capitalize on emerging trends that are not prominent or in existence. Knowing where your industry is headed, or what changes are coming ahead in your life and at your company, will help you turn these shifts into opportunities for yourself. This is one of the ways that I go the extra mile and add value wherever I go.

Going the extra mile has always helped me stand out from the pack in any organization that I have worked for. A big part of doing more than what was required of me has been asking the right questions, in anticipation of what is coming ahead, at the right time. In any project that I work on, I take stock of what everyone else is doing, and then I try to do more. I take on the responsibility for the whole project instead of just individual components of it. Being more diligent, consistently reliable, showing up earlier and staying later than everybody else, is how I show that I care a lot about the work I do. Most people do not operate in this way. The Pareto Principle, also commonly known as the "80-20 rule" (or, as I like to call it, "the law of the vital few"), explains this reality.

The "80-20 rule" is that 80 percent of the workload will be carried by 20 percent of the group. So many people fall in the 80 percent category because they are either not interested in doing the extra work or are not willing to consistently put in the level of work required to be a part of the 20 percent. Standing out and being extraordinary, at its core, is about preparedness, excellence, taking initiative, and consistency. Your drive and hustle to deliver are not only meant for your 20s or early 30s, contrary to some popular belief. It needs to be a part of the way you work in your mid-30s and 40s, too.

One of the best pieces of advice that I have ever received, about preparing for the future, is from a president of a major cable network. He suggested that I will make the most money between the ages of 38 and 45. While I previously thought that the "hustle and grind" was for the early stages of my career, I had a WMNTY (What Mommy Never Told You) moment. I realized that I really needed to work smarter and harder now more than ever. As a woman in her early 40s, I realized I was in my years of highest earning potential and I had to stand out from the pack more than ever before. The professional roles I take during this time in my career, what investments I make, and how I spend my money and time will be big contributors in setting the course for how the rest of my life will be. This advice was transformative for me.

Just when I thought I had put in the work and had gotten ahead of the game, I was reminded that this was not the time to slow down. It is like running a marathon. Even though the race has started, it doesn't really begin until the last five miles. That is when you really must dig deep and pull something extraordinary out of yourself to get to the finish line strong. Similarly, when you hit the height of your career, that's the point when you really must turn it up a few notches to get maximum results. Don't get comfortable. The work to get ahead of the game does not stop at, what you may consider being, your peak. It isn't over until it's over.

High performance is not about outperforming others, but rather it is about outperforming yourself. A marathon runner who is worried about what everybody else is doing will quickly lose sight of her own strategy. My gift is that nobody else can be me. If I am the best me there is, I will be unstoppable. The key is not to try and be ahead of others or to do more than others, but rather to differentiate yourself from everybody else. How are you different and an asset to the organization that you serve? How is your skill set uniquely developed and executed in your working environment? How are you positioning yourself with decision-makers in your organization so that your unique value proposition is seen? That is how I have managed my career.

In one of my earlier roles, as the vice president of Brand

Strategy with Combs Enterprises, I had a productive dialogue with my supervisor at the time regarding my performance. Her feedback to me was positive and I openly received input on areas of improvement. I took the opportunity to ask my supervisor for a raise in my salary. I was immediately told that an increase in monetary compensation could not be discussed at that time, as the chairman of the company did not know a lot about me or my contributions. My supervisor suggested that I figure out a way to develop a rapport with the chairman to substantiate and create visibility for the work that I did for the company.

I realized at that moment that it was my job to make my skill set and value add known to decision-makers at the company, and not my supervisor's responsibility. I took my supervisor's advice and I spoke up! In rooms where, perhaps, I would openly offer the floor for her to always speak on my behalf, I started to speak on my own behalf. I started to work closely with other leaders in the organization that had the chairman's ear. I became an expert on specific projects, making me the go-to person to present to larger groups. Over time, my corporate equity quickly became visible and began to rise. Getting ahead requires visibility and knowledge of your value add. If key influencers are not aware of what you bring to the table, they cannot reward you for it. If I had not taken steps to ensure that the chairman was aware of my contributions, I would not have had the opportunity to work as the vice resident of the chairman's office.

Your value add should not just be what you consider to be positive contributions, but they should be reflective of the expectations and standards of the organization that you work within. It is important to identify key performance indicators (KPI's) for success to know if you have delivered on them or not. You need to know what the benchmark for strong performance is before you can declare it as such. Learn what is important to the key decision-makers of the organization you work for by asking them, watching them as they work and speak, and paying attention to how people react to your work. In other words, what does a win look like for your superiors? I often even go to my friends and family for professional advice, even if they do not work in the same company or industry as me. As individuals outside of the situation, they can give me objective advice and feedback without the personal investment that I may have toward a specific outcome. You don't know what you don't know; I call these situations blind spots. It is important to engage others for feedback to discover what you don't know.

> "If key influencers are not aware of what you bring to the table, **they cannot reward you for it.**

Over the years, the lines between my personal and professional lives have blurred tremendously in more ways than just seeking professional advice from people in my personal life. There is no difference when it comes to goal setting, as my process to do so is the same in both areas of my life. My career has dictated my personal life for years now. It has become my lifestyle. I, for instance, spent four consecutive New Year's Eves working. I recognize that is not the norm for most but that became my norm in the lifestyle that I chose for myself. I also realized that was something I no longer wanted for my life and my family, and personal experiences were more valuable to me. It is in that realization that I decided that I would no longer prioritize work over personal life during that holiday and there may potentially be consequences associated with that decision. I am responsible for everything that has happened in my life. This gives me power in my decisions and my ability and drive to achieve my goals. And I set very big goals for myself.

It is important to set your, what I like to call "B.A.G." (Big Audacious Goals), high. Stretch yourself and expect greatness of yourself. You can do more than you think. Push yourself and strive for the most ridiculous goals. Don't think basic. Think B.A.G. Once you have set your big goals, think about who you need to become as a person to fulfill them. Powerful? Confident and self-loving? Forgiving? Resilient? Consistent? The answer to all of these questions is YES! Consider what is keeping you small and become the exact opposite. Understanding the tasks that need to be done to achieve goals is one thing, but you need to know what it is going to take from you personally to achieve your big dreams.

> "**I am responsible** for everything that happened in my life.

WHAT WILL YOU BE KNOWN FOR?

When I was much younger, I wanted to be known as the girl who had her life all figured out. I wore my own chip on my shoulder and had a lot to prove when I was 22 years old. I have always been fiercely independent, making my own way, and I wanted to show the world what I was made of. Growing up, so many of my peers doubted me. They thought I was delusional and sometimes looked at me like I spoke a different language. Often times I felt like I was from another planet. In my heart, I knew what I was doing and that my decisions would lead me exactly where I wanted to go. For this reason, I wanted it to be unequivocally known that I was right — I said and did the right things and that I made the right decisions.

Getting my college degree was important to me, but making money was even more important. As such, I made the decision to work on both simultaneously. In the neighborhood that I grew up in, people thought that it was cool to have a baby with their drug-dealing boyfriend and drive his Lexus sedan around town donned in the latest jewelry and fashion. It was more meaningful for me to drive my own Lexus sedan and wear expensive clothing that I paid for myself — both of which I did. I bought my own car; it wasn't a Lexus, on the contrary, it was a 1991 Volkswagen Jetta when I was 19 years old. I eventually grew my income to the point that I could buy stylish clothing because I love fashion. I also traveled extensively in my early 20s because I wanted to see the world. I took myself to Germany and France alone (I met up with my friend when I got to Germany) because I wanted to know what else was out there in the world. I had big dreams and I wanted to prove to myself that I could achieve them. I used my mind, wit, work ethic, and my passion to get what I wanted out of my life and I wanted the world to know that.

In my early 30s, I wanted nothing more than to achieve success in my career. And for me, success meant money. As a sales rep in my late 20s, I worked to no end to push through those zeros on that year-end statement. I was so intoxicated by the numbers, how much I had made, how much I had saved, how high my FICO score was. It was like a high for me. While I always envisioned myself ascending the executive ranks at some point, I never really wanted to be the one leading the pack. It wasn't about the power or the accolades for me. I wanted the monetary compensation that came with the increased responsibilities of senior leadership roles. It was always about the money for me. I also wanted to be known for redefining what a young black woman, who grew up in a rough neighborhood, was capable of. I wanted to change the perception that people had of women who looked like me or had similar backgrounds. I was not a statistic and I did not want to be considered as such. The focus of who I was became more about changing the perception of my appearance through the way I dressed, where I showed up, who I dated, and with whom I candidly shared my thoughts and experiences.

I took myself way too seriously in my 30s. I almost became a rigid mold of my own creation. This way of being also brought with it unnecessary stress and anxiety. I don't regret any of this as I do believe that it was a big contributor to my successes during that time in my life. However, I believe that I could have lightened up more. As I reflect on that period, I realize that I was still in survival mode and climbing out of the life that I could have ended up with. I was still in the headspace of navigating my way out of the cycle of poverty. I was fearful of that life. I did not want to get "caught" being pregnant, addicted to drugs, emotionally broken, or simply just getting socialized to the undercurrent of the mediocrity of inner-city life.

Today, as I write these words at the age of 42, I want to be known for many of the same things that I wanted to be known for when I was younger. However, the difference now is that it stems from a very different place. I want to redefine what it means to have it all and have a full life. While admittedly, I am a single woman who wants to be married and have children, I most definitely still have it all. I have had an abundant and full life with so many experiences that are so different from the average. I have traveled the world and visited over 50 countries, two-stepped to a track by Drake with a former president of the United States, participated as a delegate with the government of the United States in the Middle East, and planned some of the most epic parties in the past two decades. I have lived a life that even surpasses my wildest dreams.

I now want to be the woman who serves the community. I want to be known as the woman who helps others, provides guidance and mentorship, and speaks up for what matters to the community. For the first time in my life, it is no longer about the money for me. It is now about the purpose and the impact on others. I am still hardwired to think about money; this has been a fundamental part of my makeup, but the emphasis I place on it has shifted considerably. My priority now is my purpose and what my life could mean for the world at large. I am excited about this transformation and grateful for all the experiences that have led me to this place.

For a very long time, I did not know what I wanted to be known for. As a child, I used to tell my mother and godfather that I had no talent because I could not figure out what it was. They would always encourage me and say, "Don't say that honey, you do have talent. You just haven't discovered it for yourself yet — it will come." I used to see talent as something you performed, like Serena Williams on the tennis court or Will Smith on screen. I couldn't sing well, dance, or act. I did not have the physique to be a runway model. This would sometimes keep me up at night. What was I going to contribute to the world without any talent? This made me feel very insignificant for years.

I was quiet in public as a young child because I felt like I had very little to contribute. Most of the friends that I have made as an adult would laugh at the thought of a quiet version of me, but I said very little for years because I did not feel I had anything significant to contribute to a group. When I was in kindergarten, I was the valedictorian of my class and, as valedictorian, I gave my first public speech. My speech was so well-received that I was given a standing ovation by the teacher, students, and the parents of the students. I will never forget that moment. I was shocked that people were cheering for me. I remember being so scared in that moment that I began to cry when I went back to my seat. I kind of blocked that experience out of my memory for many years. Now when I reflect on the last four decades of my life, I realize that my talent was there all along.

My talent is speaking, inspiring others, and motivating people. I discovered my special gift at the age of 5 but I did not have the tools, awareness or vocabulary to identify it as such. Yet another JAY-Z quote, "Man, you was who you was 'fore you got here." (As you can see this is a reoccuring theme — get used to it — the man is a genius!)

When it comes to discovering yourself, time will always be the greatest teacher. Self-discovery is a continuous process. There are so many layers to you and it will take time to get through each layer. You are a collection of experiences, lessons, and habits and the total must be considered to really discover who you are. Have honest conversations with yourself and take responsibility for who you have become. Think about your decisions and reactions and dissect why you respond in the ways that you do. Self-assessments can be difficult, and you may not always like what you discover about yourself. Be compassionate and kind to yourself throughout this process. In the spirit of self-love, self-respect, and patience, accept who you are. Celebrate who you know yourself to be as you continue to discover who you are to become.

LEAN ON OTHERS

As someone who values and strives for independence, I have had to learn to become accustomed to leaning on others. I now have a myriad of people in my network, both personally and professionally, who I go to for support. Different people will play different roles in your life. Knowing the strengths, gifts, and roles of each person in your life will allow you to quickly know when and who to approach to help you navigate your path. Sometimes I need my mother for support, and other times I need a friend who I spiritually align with in a specific way. Sometimes I need a friend who will listen to me vent for an hour, and other times I need a colleague who I can strategize with. The best way to lean on others is to know who you can count on and for what, as well as understanding what areas of your life you may need support with.

There is an African proverb that says, "It takes a village to raise a child." Similarly, we need an even more expanded village as adults. Learning to use your network is key to succeeding. There is power in numbers, and no single part will be greater than the whole. You do not need to go through your journey alone. Different people have different gifts. What may not come naturally to you, may come naturally to another person and vice versa. People love contributing to others positively and it is fulfilling to use your talents and strengths. This is not about taking advantage of people but leveraging the human capital of your network optimally. In the same way, ensure that you make yourself available for others when they reach out to you for support. The village gives to the child and the child will eventually give back to the village as well.

When I was 24 years old, I worked for a publishing company. It was the job of a lifetime for me, at the time. Working for the company that published the magazine that I read every month was a dream job for me. After three years at this company, on the Tuesday before Thanksgiving, the company head gave notice that they were shutting the doors for good. I, along with the rest of the staff, was being laid off as the company had filed for bankruptcy. I was devastated and scared. For the first time, since I had started working full-time, I was without a job. After the news of the company's closure started to spread, to my surprise, I received four separate calls from old colleagues who became friends offering their support and assistance. I was overcome with emotion. They made me realize that I was not alone and that I did not have to figure my way out of this situation by myself. This inspired me to hit the pavement and actively search the job market. After four weeks of being laid off, I landed a sales position with the largest publishing company in the United States. I started my new job five weeks after becoming unemployed — all thanks to the love and support I received from those around me.

I was fortunate that my friends and family members offered their shoulders for me to lean on when I became unemployed as it is not an instinct for me to ask for help. Growing up, I never saw my mother, grandmother, or my aunt lean on anybody outside of our family for help. The women in my family stuck together and held each other up. The motto we lived by was "one for all, all for one."' Ironically, my close group of girlfriends is much the same. We don't hesitate to call on each other for support and creatively problem-solve together. We lean on each other. My network is a big reason why I feel safe as I navigate through the challenges, obstacles, and changes in my life.

MASTER THE ART OF GOAL SETTING

The key to mastering the art of goal setting is to get clear on what you want to achieve. I was terrible at goal setting in the early years of my career. I was not strategic in my approach at all and I would do whatever task fell into my lap. I found myself constantly working harder instead of working smarter and more efficiently. It felt a lot like I was running in circles with no finish line in sight. This approach was not serving me. It wasn't until a sales manager, at one of the publishing companies that I used to work for, shared the 3-6-9 strategy tool with me that I understood the importance of doing tasks that led to an end goal. I have been blessed over the years to be given advice by many individuals who have taught me how to effectively set my goals and achieve them.

The best and most practical advice I have ever received from a mentor was from Dr. Freda Lewis-Hall. She is an accomplished medical doctor, author, and EVP, chief patient officer of one of the largest pharmaceutical companies in the world. Though I first met her at my office in 2009 when I worked for

The Blue Flame Agency, she also happened to be the mother of one of my colleagues and good friends. The second time I met Dr. Lewis-Hall was at my friend's (her daughter's) birthday party and we were next to each other during cocktail hour waiting for the birthday girl to arrive. I had so many questions for her. I wanted to know how she achieved the top role in the company and what steps she took to get there. Her response was profound. She simply said, "Well I didn't know I was going to be here exactly, however, much like most of my accomplishments, I identified the end goal. From there, I walked back into the steps that I would take to achieve my goal. And that is how I landed the position that I am in now. I looked at all the steps that I needed to take and decided on whether I was willing to commit to them. Once I committed myself, I never let up."

It seemed so obvious when she said it, but it was profound advice for me. Hearing that advice from a very successful woman of color at the top of her organization made it real for me. I felt that it was possible for me, too. All I had to do was know where I wanted to be, map out the steps that I needed to take, and commit to those steps no matter the sacrifice. I apply this same approach as a business leader to rally my team behind a collective goal.

Just as it is important for me to personally understand why I am doing something, it is crucial for me to help my team members have this same understanding as well. I begin goal-setting conversations with my team by explaining the impact of the goals on them as individuals, and broadly for the company as a whole. Making people feel a sense of responsibility for the greater good creates a level of accountability and integrity that may not exist if they thought the impact was limited to them. My mother instilled this lesson in me from an early age.

As a single parent and the sole breadwinner of our household, my mother made sure that I understood that I had important responsibilities in our family. She set high standards for me and ensured that I knew that we were a team that had to work together. We had responsibilities of equal importance to ensure the harmony of our home. She would point out all the things that I loved about our home life: my nice pink-and-blue room, my arsenal of toys, our nice furniture, the holiday family vacations that we took, the weekend takeout food we would have, and our weekly ice cream Fridays. At the same time, my mother also pointed out the premium, the requirements, that came with having the life that we had. She would clearly relay her responsibilities as a parent and my responsibilities as a child. She brilliantly curbed any potential poor behavior and performance at school by telling me that she would have to leave work early if I got in trouble and she was called to the school. She explained that her salary would be reduced if she had to leave work early and that would mean we would have less money to buy food. It was possibly quite heavy for a 7-year-old, but it worked. I equated bad behavior at school with not having food to eat at home and that was my motivation to stay out of trouble. My why at the time was "we have to eat!" (smile).

My mother helped me understand my role and the impact I would have on our family if I did not fulfill my responsibilities. This lesson has always stayed with me. In a team setting, I think about the consequences to myself and others if I don't meet my end of the bargain. Similarly, I am also aware of the effect on my larger goals when I don't tackle my to-do lists and the necessary work to achieve my vision. Goal setting is about looking ahead while doing the work now. It is about doing the work that will put you ahead in the future.

PITTMAN'S RULES:

1. Ask yourself the question, what can I do now that will put me ahead in the future?
2. Be aware of change, accept it, and embrace it.
3. A strategy can sometimes be more valuable than a plan.
4. Set a goal and back into the road map.
5. "Man, you was who you was 'fore you got here." — JAY-Z
6. "It takes a village to raise a child" — take turns being the village and the child.
7. Use your warm network in all areas of your life but be sure to give of yourself in return.
8. Accountability and integrity are essential to success.

Chapter 6:
DEFINE AND CONTROL YOUR OWN NARRATIVE

If you don't determine your own story, somebody else will. Whether it's society trying to dictate what is acceptable or unacceptable, your parents thinking that they know what is best for you, or you are making decisions based on what you think others will think of you — too many women allow others to dictate their lives. On the path to happiness and success, you must sit in the driver's seat and hold your own. This has been my key to defining and controlling my narrative my whole life.

If you asked my mother about my early years, as early as my toddler years, she would describe me as fiercely independent. She would tell you that I never wanted anybody to dictate how I did things. I didn't want help. I was content and even determined, to find my own way. My mother often says, when I was learning to walk, that I would cry if someone tried to pick me up and get me back on my feet when I fell. I wanted to get up on my own and balance myself. While learning to walk, I would hold onto furniture for stability and, if anyone tried to move me away from the furniture I was holding to help me walk, I would burst into tears. When I was 3 years old, I recall being in the elevator of my grandmother's apartment building with my mother. I tried to press the button to go up to the fourth floor, where my grandmother lived, but I could not reach it. My mother stepped in to press the button for us. I got upset at her and smacked her hand.

"No, Mommy! Let me do the best I can do!" I shouted.

My mother calmly said, "Okay, I understand that, but you can't reach it yet."

I said, "Yes I can!" With that, I jumped as high as I could and pressed the button for the fourth floor.

I have always wanted to do things on my own, on my schedule, and my way. My former assistant, who was often asked where I was or what I was doing, once joked saying, "Leave her alone — she is her own woman!" I narrate my own story. No matter what others said or did, or what my cards read, I have always trusted myself and believed in my ability to figure it out. And I want the same for you. You will be that much prouder of your story if you hold the pen to write your own book. Throughout my life, I have witnessed too many women allowing society, friends, and family define who they are and who they should be. Women especially fall prey to the timelines that we are told to follow. The checklist of when you should finish school, start your career, get married, and have kids are real. I know this all too well as a mature and single woman. Per the conventional checklist, I should be married already with a 15- to 20-year-old child. My life should look very different from the way it looks now. This is not to say that the checklist is wrong. There is nothing wrong with it if it works for you. The primary question is not whether you are aligned with the checklist or not, but whether it makes you happy. Doing things because it's the conventional route may not be the right reason to do them. I would love to be married and have my own beautiful family, but I will not settle for that life with the wrong partner and a mediocre circumstance just for the sake of hitting that milestone. What's important is that you can look at your life and know that you are living it the way you want to, on your own terms. Life is way too short to be living on somebody else's terms. Be you and let your spirit be free. Just do you.

"Doing you" requires that you critically think about the advice given to you by others. Is the advice aligned with who you are or is it true to someone else's way of being? Is it limiting you or is it empowering you? Is the advice based on traditional social conventions or is it based on a free spirit? Early in my sales career, a male colleague in the music and entertainment industry told me that he observed that I interacted with too many men. He advised me to be careful not to build a negative reputation for myself and that I should change the way I interact with men in the industry. If I didn't, he claimed, nobody will take me seriously in the business and nobody would date me in my personal life. His comments took me by surprise and I wasn't even entirely clear about what he meant. What did "take me seriously" mean? Was he referring to my professional or personal life?

I took his advice to heart without thinking about its impact on me. I became hyper buttoned up, like a straitjacket. I knew that I needed to continue to develop and engage my client relationships in the music industry, but I needed to also figure out a way to create clear boundaries so that there would not be a false perception about my interactions. I wore corporate suits to meetings with music label executives. I carried a briefcase with me to work events at nightclubs, and I never drank or stayed out late at those events. I was all business and I became rigid all for the sake of "protecting my reputation" without ever questioning what I was protecting it from. Over the years, this way of being crippled me.

I became overly guarded and that also meant that I never allowed myself to be vulnerable. The real me is dynamic, funny, casual, fun, and easygoing. And I was none of those things for most of my career because I took advice from an illegitimate source, that wasn't true to who I was. So, what if my job in sales working in the music and entertainment industry required me to be around men often? Most of the decision makers in that industry at the time were Men, was I not supposed to do my job? Why did that have to mean that I could end up with a bad reputation? Why could that not have meant that I can successfully navigate in a male-dominated industry? Ultimately, implementing this advice hindered me in my career in the long run. Being super rigid does not work in a business environment where you need to make friends and be influential at the table. Eventually, I had to reprogram myself to balance the serious, "get it done" approach with my natural, lighter self. This required me to learn to be vulnerable.

Owning your narrative is about vulnerability and, once you become the author of your story, nobody will be able to tell it better. Creating a narrative that is true to who you are is self-empowering. It is in this state of power that you will realize that the occurrences of your life all happen for you and not to you. You needed the experiences you have had, the good and the bad, to curate the masterpiece that you are today. Trust your journey toward your truth and be patient with the process.

Discovering my story took time — a lot of time. I struggled to figure out how to differentiate between the way my life was and the way I thought it should be. I was waiting on the "should be" to manifest for so long that I was not able to see how amazing my life was. A big reason why I was challenged in this way was that I let other people's opinions influence my perception of myself. This included colleagues, family, friends, and even people who I did not know well. Several years ago, I decided that I wanted to speak on platforms about my experiences, my lessons, and share my insight to as many people as possible. To support this, I set up a meeting with a woman who worked in public relations to discuss my options. This was in 2010. I asked her how I could best pitch my narrative to various platforms.

She looked at me with a sober face and said, "But, what do you have that's worth sharing?"

Surprised, I muttered, "Excuse me? What do you mean?"

Her response, "Like, what do you have? I mean, you're not married and you don't have children. So how has your story panned out? How have you won? For you to tell a powerful story and speak as an expert, you should have had an outcome. And you haven't. I can't pitch you. There's nothing there for me to pitch."

I went dead in the face. I could not believe what I was

hearing. My life story is winning. I made it out of the projects and, at the age of 33 at that time, I was a part of the top 5 percent of income earners in America. The statistic that I became was the exact opposite of what is expected of a person from my background. But there I was sitting with this individual being told that there was nothing to share in my story because I didn't have a spouse or child. While this wasn't the first time that someone shared such disapproval of certain aspects of my life, it was the first time that I realized I had to write my own story. I should not be waiting or asking for anyone else to validate my life. I would have to develop my own narrative and create a platform for women like me. I want to be that role model for those who do not have people to look up to or speak out in support of them.

I was fortunate to have strong women in my life show me how to do this with class and grace. I was raised whole and complete. Through their daily acts, I learned how to take accountability and be the leader of my life. I learned from them that my life is the sum of a series of choices, whether right or wrong, and the key would be to take full responsibility for my choices. My mother had me when she was 21 years old and made very intentional decisions about her life after becoming a parent. She always ensured that I know I was a wanted blessing in her life and my upbringing is a testimony of this.

My mother made tremendous sacrifices in her life to raise me, including dropping out of college in her last semester of studies, but she did so to create something amazing. She wanted to create and raise a human being who would matter, count and contribute to society positively. My grandmother was disappointed that my mother made the choice to drop out of college, but she decided to do so to focus on being my mother. At that point in her life, she had to decide whether she was going to live for me or live for herself. She decided to live for me, and from that point forward, every single decision she made was based on whether it was going to benefit me. Thinking about the sacrifices that my mother made for me brings me to tears. My mother is a phenomenal woman who is committed, intentional, and she has shown me how to create my own narrative and take the utmost pride in it. She certainly took after her mother, my grandmother, in that way.

My grandmother was a young bride. She married a soldier shortly after graduating from high school. Soon after being wed, she had her first child at the age of 19 and then her second, my mother, when she was 22 years old. My grandfather's military career moved their young family to Missouri. It was 1955, she was an African-American woman raising two African-American girls living in the Midwest during times of racism and hatred in America. That in itself was a feat that required immense courage. During their time in Missouri, my grandfather developed an addiction to gambling that was impacting the family financially and emotionally. My grandmother, being the savvy woman that she was, was also an avid saver. She managed the finances for the household and would find savings wherever she could and stash money away for emergencies. One day, at the height of things going downhill for my grandfather, my grandmother made the courageous choice to take the kids and leave him.

My grandmother used her emergency fund to move her

and her toddler daughters' belongings back to New York. She set up a new life for herself and her children. For context, women in the 1950s, let alone housewives with only a high school education, did not leave their husbands and the security they provided. Women were not allowed to secure credit cards or housing loans without husbands. My grandmother was an unconventional woman who was a trailblazer in this way. She wanted her daughters to grow up in a healthy, stable, loving home environment and that was enough for her to go against the grain and rewrite her story. It didn't matter what others deemed as appropriate or inappropriate; she made the choice that she felt was best for her family. She didn't like the way her story was going to read so she took control and changed her narrative. Ultimately my grandmother raised two successful women and retired with a noted career and financial stability. We all have a responsibility to ourselves to write our own story and run our own race. Always remember to hold your own.

To hold your own is to carry your own weight and be accountable for your choices and the evolution of your life. This does not mean you should be blaming yourself for being born into the circumstances you were born into or ending up under the supervision of a bad boss, but you must sit in the driver's seat for where you go next. In the workplace, this would mean taking accountability for your wins and your failures. It means being able to back up and support your decisions, actions, and opinions. Holding your own in your career will require you to consistently deliver despite other circumstances like limited resources, business climate, or other scenarios. The will to win and succeed requires you to hold your own.

My mother and grandmother taught me how to hold my own and walk through life with confidence. Today, I am a woman who is unapologetically confident, and, because of that, I believe in myself and my decisions. You can't narrate your own story if you are unsure of it or hesitant about it. Uncertainty does not strengthen the spine, instead it weighs it down. People must believe in you and that must start with you. If you don't believe in yourself, nobody else will.

My confidence has been 80 percent of my formula to achieving success. I believe in my ability to perform and achieve. I often use history as an indicator for my future success and I can see all the challenges I have overcome and the milestones I have surpassed. Think back to a time, or times, in your life when you felt like everything was falling apart. You may have been stuck in a hard place, but you found your way out. You not only pulled through, but you triumphed. That is not by chance or luck. That was a result of your doing. Now imagine what is possible for your life. Have a broad understanding of the scope of possibilities open to you and decide for yourself how to live and operate within those possibilities. And be unapologetic about it. Being unapologetic simply means no concessions and no excuses. Period. This includes making no excuses about who you are. Being confident with your whole self, quirks and all, and being confident enough to share it with the world without any regard or care for judgment is to be unapologetic. Figure out who you are, all of it including the good and the ugly, and just embrace it. There may be things about you that you may want to refine and that's okay. What's important is that you are doing it because you believe it will make you a better version of yourself and not because that's what somebody else wants or expects of you. There are no mistakes about who you are. You were made whole and perfect from conception. Find your tribe that appreciates you and love them just the same. You don't have to win everybody over. My mother used to say, "You can please some of the people some of the time, but you can't please them all. Focus on pleasing yourself and the rest will figure it out." Promise to believe in yourself and declare it out loud.

Throughout my life, I have made bold and precise declarations about my future. There's power in words and much of that power goes untapped. Declaring a conviction out loud is to take ownership and responsibility for that choice. It is an intentional decision. Owning your decisions is the first step to living them. When I declare something out loud, I possess it in my core. It becomes that much more real to me. I assume responsibility and I nurture it to become what I envision. Declaring is a powerful way for me to make decisions and to choose.

Four years ago, I chose myself. Instead of putting everyone and everything else first, I decided to say "yes" to my needs and desires. I declared that I was priority number one and I would move anything that was getting in the way of the things that I wanted. While I still must remind myself of this declaration, I have become much better at saying "yes." Yes, go for the hike. Yes, go out to the party solo. Yes, take the vacation that you need despite the competing priorities at work. Yes, yes, yes! Make your declarations confidently regardless of what other people's opinions are about them.

When I chose to commit to being on The Singles Project, I had several friends who had very passionate views against my involvement in the show. They didn't think it was a good idea and felt that I would be making a fool of myself. They even went as far as to say that I would be ruining my career by being on the show. I heard their opinions but simply stood by my decision and powerfully chose to participate. Their opinions could not have been further from the truth. The show gave me a new level of exposure, I met a great guy who I dated for a period, and my career flourished. If I didn't believe in my bold declaration to be a part of the project, I would have let the negativity and naysayers sway me to do what they wanted me to do. I would have lost out on such an incredible experience. Like anything on television, there will be audience members who formulate opinions about you. It was important for me to be mindful of that while I was on the show, but that was no reason for me to not participate. Always remember, everyone has an opinion to share but that doesn't mean you have to listen.

It no longer matters whether you are on a television show or not because we live in the era of all things Internet and social media. It is important to understand the magnitude of what that means. Everyone in the world can see you. A simple lookup of your name on a search engine will come up with enough hits to piece together a narrative about you. Your activity on the Internet is like a red wine stain on a white rug. Remnants of the stain will always be on the rug no matter how hard you try to scrub it clean. An element of the photos you share and the messages you post will remain on the World Wide Web. Understand your responsibility and the impact of your actions online. Be mindful and intentional about the messages you share and the narrative you create online so that your story can be the one that you want it to be. What story do you want to share with the world? While it is important to express yourself to the world and be vulnerable, be mindful that we live in a digital era. You must think about the narrative that you create online and be mindful about how you portray yourself on social media. Having fun and living in the moment is important, but every picture, video, and message has a context that often can get lost in the footprint you leave behind on the Internet. Your online profile is your personification to the world. People can make an assessment about who you are based on the pictures you post on Instagram or the ideas you share on Twitter. It is important that you use social media as a positive branding tool, for the things that you want to be remembered for. I abide by these five rules to effectively manage my digital identity:

1. Pause before you post — Think about what you are posting before you post. Speaking poorly of your boss, or former boss, on social media is not wise. Going on a Twitter rant is not attractive. Sharing your drama on Facebook Live may result in you being remembered as the queen of drama. Before you post on social media, pause for just a moment and ask yourself, why am I posting or sharing this? Do I want to be remembered by this post?

2. Think about your audience — There are moments in your life that will be more suitable to share privately with your intimate family, others are best to be discussed with your best friend, and some others are most appropriate with your romantic partner. In other words, you don't have to share

every moment with your broader social media audience. Consider whether what you are sharing is relevant to your audience.

3. Evaluate the impact — Just like refraining from saying things that you may regret, you want to avoid posting things that you may regret. Use your best judgment when you are sharing on social media. Consider whether there will be long term consequences for posting about that moment in your life before you share.

4. Avoid nudes — Just don't do it. This may be personal to me and my views on public displays of nudity, but I believe some things are not for sharing and for me that includes being naked on camera. Evaluate the impact: Would your child be okay discovering these photos of you later on in life? Remember, there is no such thing as being able to permanently delete a moment once it has been shared on the great World Wide Web.

5. Be yourself and nothing else — Be authentic. Period. "Stunting for the 'gram" is fleeting and it will not make you feel better about yourself past that one moment. Be yourself and you will naturally attract a following that appreciates you. And, you will appreciate yourself more as well. Self-love includes loving the real you on social media.

Your story contributes something great to the world. Don't hesitate to share your life with others. You never know how you may impact another human being. People want to experience you. They want to hear your real story. You matter.

WHAT'S YOUR STORY?

You will discover your story when you practice getting to know yourself. It is at the crossroads between self-awareness and self-acceptance where your narrative can be found. Know what excites you, makes you afraid, and what you want to be remembered for. The answers will come with time and experience. As you mature, you will realize new information about yourself. As time goes by, you will evolve, and your story will change accordingly. Evolution is natural and should not be resisted. What is crucial is that you remain honest with yourself and stay in tune with your feelings and thoughts. it is in these moments that you discover your story is truly a liberating experience.

When you learn who you are, you have the power to choose how you want to share your story. The Queen B, Beyoncé Knowles herself, has shown us that even she has the power to share her story on her terms, despite constantly being in the public eye. Her album Lemonade debuted in 2016 and showcased a side of her and her marriage to rapper Jay-Z that had not been shared before. While the tabloids speculated rumors of cheating and distress in the couple's relationship, neither she nor her husband confirmed or denied the allegations. There wasn't a single tweet, an interview, or statement from their publicist that gave any insight into what they were dealing with. Beyoncé did share her story with the world, but she did so in the way that she wanted to. Through her music, each track on Lemonade told tales of accusations of adultery against her husband and her forgiveness of his actions. In a 2005 interview with Essence magazine, Beyoncé spoke about how she controls the narrative of her personal life. She said, "I never talk about my relationships. I only talk about them in my songwriting; otherwise things get too messy." Through her music, Beyoncé decides what she will share, how much she'll tell, and how she wants to include her fans in the evolution of her life.

The most powerful storytellers are those who engage others in the dialogue. When you address what others care about, they are more likely to be drawn to you. I am a private person and I have not been one to share stories from my personal life with anyone outside my immediate circle of friends and family — with them I am an open book. I would often go on stage and take part in panels to discuss business issues. It was in these public forums that I realized that people wanted to hear my personal stories and understand my career journey. It was this recognition that helped me engage my audience in dialogue because I learned to share with them what was important to them instead of just what was comfortable for me. My audience wanted guidance. They wanted to hear real-life stories from someone who looked like them. It was only when I started to do this that my audience grew. My story was inspiring people and all I had to do was share it authentically.

Sometimes you may not have a venue full of people to talk to from the podium. You won't necessarily have a full 45 minutes to share your story and answer questions. There will be times when you will only have 30 seconds to tell your narrative. An elevator pitch is sometimes all you have time for. Learn to effectively share your story regardless of whether you have an hour to convey it or only half of a minute. Here's how you create a powerful elevator pitch:

Step 1: Write down everything that you believe is important to you and is important about you. Don't hold back. It's best to lay it all out so that you can think about it. If you have a hard time getting started on this step, just think of five words that describe your story. For me, my five words are:

Resilient because I have overcome every obstacle that I have encountered in my life.

Dynamic because I am constantly evolving and growing. I have broad perspectives that have given me an expanded view of the world.

Authentic because everything I do is from my heart. I say what I mean, and I do what I say.

Unapologetic because I am whole, complete and proud of all that is me. I don't make excuses for any part of my being. I am not sorry to be me exactly as I am.

Unique because I'm different. I don't fit stereotypes or societal molds. I am the only me there will ever be.

Step 2: Go over your notes and eliminate or combine redundant statements.

Step 3: Read your notes repeatedly. I recommend reading it seven to10 times. Process them and reflect on the statements each time that you read them.

Step 4: Once you have considered what is most important to you, reduce it to two to five sentences and combine them into one flowing narrative. You should be able to describe who you are and what is important to you in 30 seconds or less.

Step 5: Read over your amended elevator pitch and memorize it. Learn to share it with passion and enthusiasm.

As my life and interests have changed over the years, my elevator pitch has also evolved. I regularly review and adjust my narrative. My elevator pitch is:

I exist to create a world that offers abundant possibilities for myself and those around me. Doing well by doing good is my daily mission.

FAKE IT TILL YOU MAKE IT

You don't know what you don't know, and you may only learn by doing. Therefore, even if you are completely unsure of yourself, do it anyway. In other words, fake it till you make it and eventually you'll learn. Every time that you take on a new role and start a new job, there will be an element of faking it until you get accustomed and go through the learning curve. No matter how much experience or knowledge you may have, at the end of the day, every new situation is just that — it is new to you. Trust what you already know and believe in your ability to adjust and learn. What is foreign will eventually become familiar.

One of the most foreign experiences I have had is taking part in the reality television show *The Singles Project* as one of the single women. The purpose of the show was to show how young, professional, single men and women date. My mission for participating was larger than that. I wanted to dispel stereotypes about women who looked like me and show the world how black women carry themselves. I was excited about my purpose on the show but still very much afraid. The whole opportunity was so new to me and it was unlike anything else I had experienced.

I remember my first day on set like it happened yesterday. In my mind, I kept thinking about whether I had made the right decision or not. *What was I doing on a reality TV show? How was this all going to turn out?* On the first day, we did part of our filming outdoors. The weather must have been 100 degrees that day and I was worried that my makeup was going to separate from my face and my hair was going to get messy from the heat. I wanted to show up impeccably and represent well for women of color who don't get featured on TV often. It was a "fake it till you make it" moment for me because I had to deliver even though I had never had a role on a show before. I had to be my best self at that moment even if I didn't think I could do so. Just because I didn't know everything about being on reality TV didn't mean that I was not worthy of that experience. I simply leaned into the experience and brought with me all the tools and knowledge I had developed throughout my life. I trusted myself to make it a positive experience regardless of how I felt in the beginning. Ultimately it was a huge success. I used my life tool kit, took a situation by the horns, and made it a win for myself.

Life throws curve balls and new experiences at you and you must learn to maneuver them. The ability to be agile is a skill that is acquired with practice. Learn to fake it till you make it. Success is imminent if you stay in the game long enough to master it.

PITTMAN'S RULES:

1. Write your own narrative. Don't wait for others to validate your choices.
2. Take responsibility for the choices you make.
3. Be mindful of what you share and with whom YOU share it.
4. Take advice from others with caution.
5. Make your own life checklist.
6. Make no concessions and make no excuses. Unapologetically be yourself.
7. Say "yes" to your own needs and desires. Stop making yourself priority number two.
8. Fake it till you make it. Eventually, you will no longer have to fake it.

Chapter 7:
SET THE BAR HIGH

Women are getting different results than men. Research has shown that, as the years go by in women's careers, there is a steady decline in their participation in senior management roles.[1] I have mentored and given advice to many women throughout my career and I have often heard statements like, "Oh, that's impossible to do," "I want to have a family at some point and I have to prepare for that," and "I'm not ready." I have seen too many women set the bar too low for themselves based on the limitations they or others have set. Oftentimes these limitations are born because of fear. [1]

Here's the reality: Unreasonable goals require unreasonable staying power and belief in self. What do the likes of Lewis Latimer, Madam C. J. Walker, Thomas Edison, the Wright brothers, Albert Einstein, Oprah Winfrey, and Steve Jobs all have in common? They were unreasonable in their pursuit of out-of-this-world and totally unthinkable goals that created groundbreaking results. What you believe you can do is ultimately what you will do.

Women tend to play a small game when it comes to their professional ambitions. For some of us, we only ask for what we think we can achieve. I have found that men have less issue with asking for what they want. They are taught to hunt and go after their prey. They learn to eat what they kill and to provide. It is likely that through this evolution, they more naturally go after and ask for what they want, whether they deserve it or not. I experienced a few examples of this in the early years of my career. I did not know how to effectively negotiate, and I had no

1 https://www.nytimes.com/2018/05/23/upshot/why-the-number-of-female-chief-executives-is-falling.html

idea what I should ask for in terms of monetary compensation. I didn't believe that I had options, let alone know what my options were. If it weren't for Steven Gold, my boss at the time, I would not have known or stood up for the realm of possibilities that were available to me. He was the first of a few to show me how to negotiate and ask for what I was worth. This encouraged me to push past what I thought I had to settle for and raise my hand to advocate for myself.

Fast-forward five years. After a successful first stint in the publishing world, I was headhunted for a role in another publishing company — the second largest publishing company at the time. It was during this experience that I learned to question whether I was short changing myself and should seek more than what I thought I could get. During the hiring process, Keith Clinkscales, my former employer and mentor, had been contacted as a reference by the hiring company's director of Human Resources. During his communication with the company looking to hire me, he became aware that they were looking to close the deal with me. They really wanted to hire me. At the time, I was honored just to be considered by this company and didn't even consider how to value myself. I did not know what to ask for.

Fortunately for me, Keith saw what I was about to do to myself and stepped in to help. He sat me down and had a detailed conversation about what my ask could be. He dissected every part of the hiring company's communication to clearly deduce what their need was. I was amazed at his ability to use their communication to decipher the opportunity in front of me.

Keith then proceeded to say, "How much do you want?"

My response, "Umm, I don't know. Is it even my choice?" "I mean, if I get what I am currently making, I would be honored considering the status of this company."

"Ericka, stop. I don't have time for this. What do you want? Everyone knows what they want, Ericka."

I said, "Honestly, I'm happy with what I already have. It is already more than I was expecting to begin with."

Keith, trying to be as patient as possible, said, "Look, this is a new ball game. You are now playing with bigger fish. They want you, but you don't need them. They need you! So, what do you want?!"

I didn't know how to answer Keith's question. I already thought I was getting all that I could get. It seemed inappropriate to ask for much more. I thought that overstepping my boundaries would hinder the offer and my chances at getting it. I thought it might reflect my lack of expertise in the process. I told Keith that I genuinely didn't know how to answer his question and proceeded to ask him what he would ask for. I recall the process being so foreign to me. I remember not knowing where to begin or even how to value myself, their needs, and the value of the overall opportunity. What factors needed to be considered to bring me to the outcome that I desired? I did not have the answer to my own question, so I asked Keith. I decided that I would use his response as a frame of reference to explore.

Keith told me what he would ask for and I almost gasped. It was way more than what I would have ever asked for. It was about 50 percent more than what I had in mind. I almost cringed thinking about the difference. He rationalized for me why he would ask for the much larger amount by listing several attributes that I would bring to the table and the kind of value that I would bring to the organization. After convincing me that I had every right to ask for a higher salary, I settled on an amount that was two-thirds of what he recommended. I still felt that the amount was outrageous, and it took so much courage for me to agree to the amount. Even with encouragement and championing, I still did not think I was good enough or that I was worth the dollar figure I was going to ask for. I was playing a small game and setting the bar far too low for myself.

Keith still wasn't convinced. He said, "Ericka, are you sure that is all you want to ask for? I'm going to call back their director of HR and tell her the amount that you are thinking. And I'm only going to call her back once."

I replied, "Yes! That would be more than enough."

He said, "Okay, stay put in your office. I'm going to call her and then I'll call you to give you an update."
As I waited to hear the outcome of the conversation, I kept doubting myself. I couldn't believe what I had done. Asking for such an exorbitant amount of money was going to cost me the job opportunity. What had I done? I have asked for too much, and now they are never going to hire me. Who do I think I am? I'm a young black girl and this major beauty magazine targeted

white American women. They are never going to make this kind of investment in me!

As I sat in my office wallowing in my own self-defeating thoughts, my phone rang. It was Keith. He told me that they were going to offer me $110,000, an amount that was already 15 percent more than what I was making at the time. While I would have accepted that amount, Keith responded with, "Well she is looking for $125,000. The amount Keith indicated was 32 percent more than my salary at the time and it was not the amount that I agreed to with him. He asked for much, much more. The director of Human Resources from the hiring company told him that the amount he indicated was above their budget and she would have to get senior management's approval for it. I was furious. Not only had I allowed this man to negotiate an amount that was not the one we had agreed to, but I felt like he sabotaged my opportunity altogether.

"Why would you do that? They were already offering more than what I am making."

He cut me short and said, "Ericka! Stop it! This is a negotiation. It's a game. It's all a game! Think about it. If she came out of the gate and offered more than either of us were even thinking of asking for, then she would have no additional room to play with. We know her hand. She has more to negotiate with. She would not have gone back for approval. Relax. You're in a good place. Just wait it out."

It took everything out of me to wait patiently and not call

the hiring company myself. It was at the end of that day that Keith called me. He heard back from the director of Human Resources and they had agreed to the 32 percent increase and offered me the job! I couldn't believe it. In less than 24 hours, I got a 32 percent salary increase. Over and above the additional financial compensation, I learned an important lesson through the entire experience. WMNTY?: To play the game is to know your worth, calculate your opposition's hand, and most importantly be brave enough to set the bar high. You will not strive high if your bar is not high. I learned to get more than I thought I could get. I became ambitious in more ways than one.

Even now, almost 20 years later, my ambition continues to evolve. Growing, and learning to expect more of yourself, is an ongoing process. I am an overachiever by nature. My desire to perfect everything I do has kept my ambition in overdrive. While I don't benchmark myself against others, I am constantly trying to be a better version of myself. There is something in my spirit that tells me that my story is grandiose and is meant to be shared with the world. I am often thinking about what else I can do to get to where I am meant to be. This way of thinking pushes me to want more, and subsequently, I end up doing more. The reality is that human beings, in general, strive for less than they have the potential to fulfill. In other words, we shortchange ourselves.

We are all born with a clean slate and are destined for greatness. Somewhere along the way in our journey, some people lose their sense of greatness, and others retain it forever. We meet people, have certain experiences, hear other people's opinions, and we start living a mediocre way of life. This way of being keeps us small. We start to think I can't, I'm not capable, and that's not for me. For me, the truth as I see it is that we are made in the image of God, so how could we not be perfect as created? Don't hold back in life. Invest in yourself and spend time focusing on fulfilling your purpose instead of ignoring or neglecting it. I know in my gut that I am meant for a bigger purpose and, no matter how hard I try to put it out, that fire continues to light me up. It is what I am on this planet to fulfill. If you don't know what your purpose is, your number-one priority should be to find out.

Mentors have been instrumental in my career. Especially in my early professional years, I had very little insight on how to effectively navigate the complexities of a workplace. My mentors coached and helped guide me as I tried, failed, and tried again, eventually leading to success. They were my sounding board. I have never taken their impact on me for granted and I strive to be the same for others who seek mentorship from me. I have, and continue to, mentor many women in my career. The most common statement I hear from most of the women I meet is, "I don't know what I want to do, but let me tell you what I have done." They are looking without any inclination as to what they are searching for. Too many people chart their journey without mapping their destination. The problem is that we spend too much time on what happened and what went wrong instead of focusing on what's next. Women, especially, often get caught in the former rather than the latter.

On a trip to Miami, I was with a few girlfriends having girl talk over drinks. Our late afternoon conversation carried into the evening. We talked about everything from men, work, dreams, failures, and more. As we sat there conversing, we were interrupted by a man who must have been listening in on part of our conversation.

He said, "Wait, wait, wait. Hold up. You want to know what the problem is with you women? Here's the thing, I listened to what you were talking about. The issue is that you are so busy being worried about your problems that you are not looking for solutions. Who even cares what happened. It's all about what's next." He looked at us for a minute, smiled and said, "I'm done here. Thank me later."

We mockingly thanked him for his advice but instantly realized the truth in his words. My girlfriends and I kept talking about what happened so much that we weren't focused enough on the what now. To this day, I am constantly reminding myself to put the past aside and concentrate on what is to come. What's next is far too important to not give it the time and consideration it deserves. Even now, his words replay in my mind as a reminder. *Who cares what happened! Focus on what is next, Ericka!*

A mentorship relationship is not forever. Sometimes your mentor moves on due to life changes or other priorities, or you outgrow them. The relationship could last five years, two years, or even just a season. It is therefore especially crucial that you optimize the opportunity that you have with them. When you meet with a mentor, don't focus on the past. Use the valuable time you have with them to talk about what is next for you. The questions you should be focusing on are: What do you want? Where do you want to go? What are you trying to accomplish next? What does your immediate future look like? What does your long-term future look like? When you cut out the mind clutter and the extra noise from your thoughts, you can focus on the things that you can impact.

The past is done, and it cannot be changed. The future, on the other hand, can be influenced by you. Once your mind starts focusing on what is next, your conversations with your mentor(s) will be more like this: How do I prepare for where I ultimately want to end up? How can I clarify my future goals? How do I map out my path toward my goals? Can you share similar success stories that ended up at the destinations I want to go to? Your goal should be to figure out what's next for you and be prepared to communicate to others how they can support you in getting there.

> "Who cares what happened! **Focus on what is next!**

There have been many people who have supported me throughout my career. I have had many powerful mentors including Sean Combs. He has taught me to utilize every tool in my toolbox to make even the impossible of futures possible. I have learned from him to go after what I want and achieve the dreams that I want for my life. You don't have to take no for an answer if no is not the answer you want. Think of no as the beginning of negotiations or a plan B. Setting the bar high is not just about bold declarations, but it is about diligence and fine execution of a well-crafted plan.

The tools in your toolbox develop when you process and evaluate everything that has occurred in your life — your experiences, feelings, and lessons. All things, good or bad, in your life have happened for you and not to you. When you become and remain a victim, you give away too much of your power. The lessons we learn and the skills and knowledge we gain from every circumstance is a tool that can be used in the future. How you apply these utensils will shape your ability to make things happen and navigate any situation or circumstance.

I loved my hometown, and, for the longest time, I could not even imagine living anywhere but New York. However, I knew that to reach my goals, I had to forgo being limited by geography. I often told friends, family, and mentors that I would be open to moving outside of New York for the right job and the greater good of my family. Moving to Los Angeles for one role, ultimately led me to the opportunity to be the chief marketing officer for a premium water company. I not only, surprisingly to myself, ended up loving life in Los Angeles, but I also achieved my dream to be the head of the entire marketing division. I knew my vision for my career, I created a framework to achieve it, and I backed into the steps to get there.

The shift to my new life in Los Angeles was difficult and the experience has been consistently evolving. After adjusting to a bicoastal lifestyle, and settling into a new personal life schedule, I transitioned into a new job at a new company with a very different culture. I had to get accustomed to an almost foreign city, I created a brand-new home for myself, and I had to build my professional colleague and friend circle network there from scratch. I had to use the tools in my toolbox to successfully back into this plan.

Big or small, at their core all our plans are just a series of combined choices. I made a choice to move to Los Angeles and accepted a senior leadership role. I then had to make the very risky choice of leaving the culture of the company I had worked with for 7 1/2 years to take the new role as chief marketing officer. I chose to lease a furnished apartment when I initially moved because I was so sure that it was not going to be a permanent change. As I began to find comfort in my new environment, I decided to commit to a long-term lease in Los Angeles resulting in me solidifying my move there. The decisions you make are often not isolated. Each one is connected to another, and that to another, ultimately all connecting back to your plans. Your choices start with who you are in relation to who you want to become.

In simple terms, Be + Do = *Have.*

Have an honest conversation with yourself about what it will take for your current self to get to where you want to be. Once you have self-reflected and thought about what you will give up and the actions you will take to achieve your goals, it is all about doing the work consistently to achieve the results that you want. It is in the thick of these actions where the greatest challenges lay. When you are tired, frustrated, upset, heart-broken, financially broke, or despondent — *do you have what it takes to be who you need to be to keep pushing forward?* The real challenge is in making the choice to keep doing the work regardless of whether you feel like doing it or not. I have yet to figure out a shortcut to success. It requires huge amounts of staying power and alignment with your moral compass.

For the most part, we know in our hearts what is right or wrong. It is important to always ask yourself, *is this the right thing to do? Should I eat this burger? Should I give 150 percent to do this project well? Should I have unprotected sex with this person? Should I sleep in today? Should I call in sick today? Should I go to class?* With each response, or choice, comes a subsequent question: *Is my response in line with my integrity? In other words, will I be compromising my morals and values by making this choice?* Any choice you make is a decision, and any decision you make is a commitment. At its core, it is about doing and being what you said you were going to be and do. Your word is your precursor to action. There is a responsibility that each of us must bear for birthing ideas and putting them out into the universe.

Committing to my word, for myself especially, has been an area that I struggle with. I don't always live up to my own self-commitments. I am, too often for comfort, flaky with my own time. I lounge more than I should. I binge-watch television sometimes and eat way too much junk food. I can be an annoy-ing complainer. I sleep in when I should be out doing something meaningful. I don't read as many books as I want to. I say I am going to do things and then I just don't do them and offer myself no consequences for my actions or inactions. It is virtually self-abuse. I can sometimes be disrespectful to myself. I have realized in recent years that I have an opportunity to be truer to myself. I can stand to work on my integrity for my own word. I can sometimes make it okay to let myself down, these traits are not consistent with self-love.

I can be completely inconsistent at times. I'm like a cheetah — I can run fast, likely faster than most others. However, I don't run for long. I do a great job, but I usually only last for a short period of time. I am a sprinter who gases out, not a marathoner. I love to start, but I get bored when finishing, often getting distracted along the way. The manuscript for this very book was four years in the making until I finally got help to get coached to the finish line. My inconsistency to myself has been my hidden secret that has plagued me in too many ways. I allowed it to impact my life for far too long.

I now live with a new commitment to set the bar higher for loving myself. True self-love means having the utmost commitment to being what I need to be to live my best life. It means taking the time to clarify what I want for my future, waking up early to meditate and self-reflect, prioritizing my health and wellness, and committing to experiences over things. I no longer waste energy fighting the way the world is. I allow myself to accept and align with the world as it is instead of resisting it based on how I think it should be. Honoring my commitments to myself and having integrity for my word has strengthened my feelings of self-worth.

ALL THINGS BUILD ON THE FOUNDATION OF INTEGRITY

Integrity is one of the most important traits we need to live our best lives, both professionally and personally. When we think about integrity, or the lack thereof, we often think about cheating, lying, and stealing, but it is much more than that. Integrity is also about taking ownership of your actions and taking accountability when it is yours to take. As well, it is also very much about staying true to your word and doing what you said you would do, whether it is a commitment you make to another person or to yourself.

Have you ever met someone who seems to always get the interesting opportunities at work, the invite to cool parties, and they are just all around happy in life? They are not unicorns and they haven't been given any special privileges that the rest of us cannot access. These are individuals who can be counted. They have a high order of integrity and, therefore, they will always do what they say they will do, they will show up, and they will complete assignments when they said they will complete them. They can be trusted to be exactly who they said they will be and, therefore, they are ultimately rewarded.

At its core, integrity is very much about taking responsibility. Laying blame on others or finding any excuse to justify your action or inaction, is not integrous. I have learned over the years that integrity should be the baseline for anything and everything that I do. When I am out of integrity, I stop and reflect on the situation and my way of being in that circumstance. This allows me to see where the breakdown occurred, and course correct from there. I have learned to not be so harsh on myself. With patience and a commitment to restoring integrity where I have lost it, I am able to come back to my baseline while being kind to myself. I am human, and my ego can and will get the best of me at times. What is important though is that I recognize when it does and reground myself. Self-reflection and frequent check-ins with myself have been crucial to the evolution toward my highest self.

Your most important goal should be to continuously grow and be a better version of yourself, while knowing that you will make mistakes every now and then. Having integrity is not about being perfect or "on point" every single time. In its purest form, it is about doing your best while understanding that breakdowns will occur, but equally prioritizing the restoration of integrity when necessary. Restoring integrity is not a simple apology to yourself or others. It is also not accepting what happened and moving on. To truly restore integrity, you need to digest and genuinely feel the impact of your decision on yourself and those around you. With this understanding, you must then recommit to a new way of being and share it with those whom you have impacted through your actions.

There is an old saying that says, "Winners never cheat, and cheaters never win." This means that you cannot truly win when you do so by cheating others or being out of integrity in your pursuit to win. You will not be happy with yourself knowing you have compromised people along the way. No matter who you are or how you justify your actions, you will be haunted by the demons of being out of integrity at some point in your life. There is no way to truly escape harming yourself or others without restoring integrity the right way. Being successful is important, but so is being a whole and complete human being. Consistently lacking integrity will put you on the fast track to be an empty vessel.

Always begin by asking yourself, who am I being and why am I doing what I'm doing? If you don't like your answers, then re-evaluate what you are about to do and take a different action. While self-awareness and forgiveness are powerful tools to help you reset after being out of integrity, it is important to take ownership of the impact you caused because of it. Forgiveness on its own is a mediocre action, however, forgiveness combined with restoration of integrity is superior behavior. Set the bar higher by being superior in your conduct and not mediocre.

BE A FAN OF CONSISTENT WORK AND PERSEVERANCE

They say it takes 10,000 hours to master a skill or talent. That works out to approximately 417 days. Even if you devote three hours a day to an area of your life that you want to improve, it will only take you a little over nine years to be extraordinary at something. Three hours a day may seem like a lot, but it still gives you 21 hours a day to do anything else that you need to do or want to do. Whether you spend three hours a day on your craft, or 30 minutes a day, it is a question of *how much do you want it? How hungry and determined are you?* There is nothing that supersedes consistent work and perseverance, even when superior talent exists.

Megastar Will Smith, whose success in Hollywood has spanned over two decades, has famously said, "And where I excel is ridiculous, sickening, work ethic. You know, while the other guy's sleeping, I'm working." Smith credits his success to his willingness to go the extra mile and work harder than anyone else, even after reaching the pinnacle of his career. Sure, he may have been born with talent, much like many others, but what separates him is his commitment to the process of acquiring and strengthening his skills. Smith is not unique in this regard among highly successful individuals. Oscar-winning actor Denzel Washington has spoken of taking acting lessons to strengthen his craft, even after winning the highest award in show business. Business tycoon and self-made billionaire Mark Cuban credits his immense success to having an immense work ethic, one that has remained the same since his early job as a bartender. Cuban has been quoted saying, "It's not about money or connections — it's the willingness to outwork and outlearn everyone else." Their stories are inspirational, but they don't have to be anomalies. We too can achieve anything we want through consistency, outworking and outlearning everyone else.

My entire life has been the result of utmost hard work and perseverance. It could have been easier to make decisions for the moment and not think about the long-term impact. I could have run around distracted by the boys in the neighborhood; I'm sure that would have been fun at the time, but I chose to study and excel at school instead. It would have been easier to not put myself out to the world, and let my false negative beliefs surrounding being a black girl from the projects hold me back, but I took the difficult road of overcoming my mental blocks to get exposure to new environments. The culmination of who I am is a combination of decisions that were not easy. They were often the unpopular choices at the time, and it took discipline and a strong work ethic to see them through.

I am a fan of hard work and perseverance, but both qualities for me culminate to working smart. Knowing that you are doing all that you can to achieve an outcome, and are consistent in your pursuit to achieve it, is key to being successful. Don't give up until it is done, no matter how long it takes to achieve it. Early on in my life I had to subscribe to the ability to work toward my goals despite the obstacles in my way. I have been ridiculed and judged for not being like the norm. I have been ostracized and objectified in the process of focusing on my own goals. I have made peace with these moments and those who have spoken about me negatively because not being the norm and focusing on what's most important is what has brought me success.

The foundation of hard work and perseverance is integrity. When you take ownership and responsibility for completing a task or a commitment to yourself, you will do all that is required to get it done. It is about bringing your best self to a situation, ultimately allowing you to achieve positive results.

PITTMAN'S RULES:

1. Unreasonable goals require unreasonable staying power and belief in self.
2. Be your biggest advocate. Negotiate. And don't settle.
3. Put your past aside and concentrate on what is to come.
4. All things build on the foundation of integrity.
5. Hard work and perseverance supersede talent.
6. To thine own self be true.

HOW TO DOMINATE IN A MALE-DOMINATED INDUSTRY

"I believe that the next 20 years will bring with it the greatest evolution and progress made by women all around the world."

I love fashion. I am known to always have my hair done. I prefer it in loose waves with a bit of wave at the end. My nails are manicured, always. I wear makeup and I love to rock a bright red lip. I'll wear a power suit to work if I feel like it, but I am just as comfortable sitting at the boardroom table in a great fitted dress. Unless I am running around planning an event, a pair of high stiletto heels is my go-to. Years ago, my current approach to style may have made me nervous. My priority would have been to look the part, hair pulled back with a square suit on, to fit in with the men instead of dressing in the way that most reflected me. Today, I take my whole self to do business just the way I am. I have learned that bringing my feminine energy is precisely what is needed to stand out and succeed.

You don't have to compromise who you are to stand out as a woman in a male-dominated industry, organization, or occupation. Bring your feminine energy to the table because it is often lacking in much of the corporate world. As women, our natural way of being is a tremendous asset to any organization. We are, in many cases, born multitaskers, we are empathetic, patient, and organized. Women often can see multiple aspects of a decision and understand how one will affect the other. Research has shown that leadership teams make smarter, more informed decisions when there is a greater proportion of senior female leaders in an organization. We don't need to compete with men or assume their personas in the workplace because what is missing is the feminine energy that only we can bring.

According to Catalyst, a global non-profit founded in 1962 that is working to build workplaces that work for women, male-dominated occupations are defined as those that have 25 percent or less women occupying them.[22] In other words, these are environments where women are significantly outnumbered, making it difficult for them to navigate and progress in their careers. In these spaces, masculinity and masculine stereotypes are more likely to be reinforced and accepted as the norm. In the United States in 2017, less than 7 percent of the full-time roles in male-dominated occupations were held by women, despite them having higher achievements in education than men.[3] My own career resembles these statistics, having worked mostly in male-dominated environments.

Since the beginning of my career, I have always worked in organizations where most staff and management were men. That was unplanned and unintentional, but I was not dissuaded to join those organizations just because I would be outnumbered there as a woman. Despite being the minority, I managed to outperform many others and was promoted multiple times throughout my career. Each of my previous experiences were fantastic opportunities and I grew as a professional because of them. It did not occur to me to be afraid to enter those spaces and you should not be afraid either.

Fear is just fear. At the end, anything that you are afraid of can only be dealt with head on. You must push through. *Is it easy?* No. *Is it worth it?* Yes. *Will you want to quit part way through?* Maybe, but that doesn't mean you have to stop midway. I became more driven to succeed because I was different, an anomaly, in many of the environments that I was in. I had to

2 https://www.catalyst.org/knowledge/women-male-dominated-industries-and-occupations
3 https://www.catalyst.org/knowledge/women-male-dominated-industries-and-occupations

push myself that much more to accomplish what the men at the company were able to achieve with less hard work and effort than I'd shown.

Often finding myself as the odd one out was challenging at times. I had to deal with my own negative self-talk, let alone negativity from others, and even the imposter syndrome. Feeling like I am an imposter had me persistently afraid that I may be exposed as a fraud. I struggled with this for many years. I would feel inadequate despite having the results and successes to show for myself.

Every time I've entered a new role in my career, I became overwhelmed by the idea of all the things I don't know about that role. Those thoughts made me feel like perhaps I had bitten off more than I could chew, or the decision to hire me was a mistake. I learned to work through these self-defeating thoughts by catching myself in my pattern and reminding myself of all that I have proven and am capable of. I literally look myself in the mirror, laugh, and say, "Don't believe me just watch!" Reminding myself of who I am gives me the clarity of mind to take a very pragmatic approach to going through the learning curve. I familiarize myself with my new role, which includes taking account of all the things I think I may not know about the position. From there I cross-reference the experiences in my toolbox to find my transferable skills and knowledge. I then look at my social capital to identify individuals who can support me with the areas that are not as familiar to me. Once I go through my process, which starts by putting an end to the negative feelings I harbored about myself, I no longer feel like an imposter.

I have learned to deal with my feelings by regularly taking a self-inventory. Identifying my wins, big and small, and appreciating who I am has been pivotal for my confidence. I had to constantly remind myself that I belonged, even if the environment around me looked drastically different from me. Through my experiences, I learned that I didn't have to be like a man to operate with them effectively.

> "I learned that I **didn't have to be like a man** to operate with them effectively.

Being the only woman in the boardroom did not mean that I had to fit anyone's preconceived notions about how a woman should be in such an environment. Society conditions all of us, both men and women, to conform to the roles that are traditionally expected of us. This is a reality that we must acknowledge so that we can consciously manage it. Pretending or ignoring that gender roles are not directly and indirectly reinforced in the spaces we operate in, does not serve us. *Have you ever noticed that most often it is women who assume the role as the minute taker in meetings at work? Or that it is usually the women who plan the charity fundraisers and team building activities? And how about all the office talk of a female leader being "bossy" or "aggressive" when she's just speaking her mind and trying to get things done for the betterment of the organization? Why are our standards so different for men and women?* We cannot allow subjective roles and norms to dictate how we act or who we can be.

Women are not second-class to men. We are not inferior to them and they are not inferior to us. However, when we do the things that men do, there is a different standard placed on us. This unfairness and double standard in relationships is addressed in the single "Like a Boy" by R&B songstress Ciara. In her line, "Sometimes I wish I could act like a boy," she presents the idea of women assuming the gender norms men have the privilege of enjoying. The unfairness could be removed if it were accepted for women to do the things that men get to do and be the kinds of people that men get to be. The double standard between men and women is also clearly seen in the workplace as well.

Women have every right to speak up and be the leaders that we want to be — no matter the style of leadership or how "aggressive" it could be perceived. When a man, especially a Caucasian one, is direct and forward in his demeanor, it is labeled as "leadership." For women, of any race, on the other hand, the same character is often viewed as "bossy" or "aggressive."

I remember taking on the role of vice president of the chairman's office at Comb's Enterprises and, after a week in the role, I was contacted by one of my male counterparts who chastised me for my delivery of a presentation. He couched his words as "giving me words of advice," but his comments were condescending and demeaning. He told me that I was like a "bull in a fine china shop" and that my presence was coming off too strong. My response was to laugh at the suggestion. I found it amusing that he considered my male counterparts fragile like "china." I asked him, "Who he considered the fine china to be, and how would anything other than a bull make things happen? If I were a man, would you be asking me to be gentler with my colleagues?" He admitted that he would be having a very different conversation with men, but his advice was "for the success of my role and it was sincere." I didn't take his advice for what he intended, and that was to encourage me to become gentler but learned what some of the obstacles would be that I would face in my role. While I was dismissive at first, I ultimately used the information as a tool to navigate how I would communicate with the team moving forward. The fragility of the egos in question aka "the fine china" was the leverage I would use to navigate my own success.

This is the reality for too many black women in the workplace, especially the corporate world. Being a strong and confident black woman at work gets you labeled as the "aggressive lady" or worse, "the angry black woman" even if there are men in the organization who display the same characteristics. The challenges faced by women, especially women of color for whom the intersection of race and gender creates more obstacles, are barriers to their growth. They are almost forced to limit their leadership and change who they are to be malleable to what is palatable in the organization.

In 2018, the Harvard Business Review showcased a study led by Maura Cheeks and Dr. Elizabeth Wolfe Morrison examining the impact on women of color who work in environments where the majority of the team does not look like them. Highlighted in the study was a phenomenon called "code-switch-ing"[4] which saw the women of color struggle with embracing the dominant culture in the organization they worked for. It was both a mental and emotional strain to "code-switch" because they felt that they had to live up to an image that was not authentic to them. It wasn't just faking it till you make it, it was pretending to make it and then feeling compelled to continue to pretend even after you made it. Having diversity in an organization is not about hiring more women and people of color to meet a target, but it is about hiring diverse candidates and allowing them to be different and showcase their diversity.

At its core, diversity is about having the best of everything and together, they make a strong combination. For example, the best financial and investment advisers would tell you to diversify your portfolio to spread the risk and reap the most optimal portfolio growth. This means that to diversify your portfolio, you go across categories of companies, sectors, and even regions. Therefore, from a human capital perspective, diversity means having a balanced combination of women, men, non-binary genders, Caucasians, people of color, and those who identify as LGBTQUIA. By having diversity in their workforce, organizations will reap the benefit of having a breadth of perspectives and experiences at their decision-making and problem-solving tables. It is the most risk-averse option and has the highest reward potential.

To innovate, organizations need to have fresh perspectives and an evolving vision. In a 2018 *Fast Company* article titled "Want a More Innovative Company? Simple: Hire a More

4 https://hbr.org/2018/03/how-black-women-describe-navigating-race-and-gender-in-the-workplace

Diverse Workforce," writer Ben Schiller says that diversity is crucial to helping a company become more innovative, and therefore, more successful.[5] In a 2017 study conducted by McKinsey & Company, the data showed that the companies that had the most gender diversity on their leadership teams were 21 percent more likely to experience above average profitability.[6] Despite research showing that diversity is correlated to the success of a company, women continue to be underrepresented in many industries.

To diversify an organization that is male-dominated, it starts with one hire. One by one, as the opportunity to hire arises, leaders in an organization need to consider whether the individual they are hiring is bringing a perspective that is missing in their boardrooms or are they bringing more of what already exists. To bring more women into an organization, you start where you can. When a woman is hired, she will start to identify and connect with other women who are already working for the organization or are considering joining the company. Female talent will naturally gravitate toward the hiring company and feel comfortable joining that workspace.

The reality is that many people hire through their own warm networks. There is comfort and security in doing this. Hiring someone with a great profile, who also comes with a recommendation from a trusted source, is more comfortable than hiring someone who only has a strong résumé. An organization dominated by Caucasian men will continue to mostly only see

5 https://www.fastcompany.com/40515712/want-a-more-innovative-company-simple-hire-a-more-diverse-workforce
6 https://www.mckinsey.com/business-functions/organization/our-insights/delivering-through-diversity

Caucasian men occupying the roles in the establishment. Having more women in the executive suite with decision-making responsibilities will create the kinds of conditions, like mentorship opportunities and familiarity, that will attract more women. Until such time that male-dominated spaces become diverse, women in those environments need to learn to effectively navigate them, including being mentored by men.

I have had many male mentors who have taught me a lot, especially early on in my life and career. Even as a child, I had major male influences around me. My godfather Joe was the first man who was nurturing and caring towards me. He would cook for me when I stayed with him, including making my favorite dishes for Sunday dinner, and gently comb my hair for me. Through my relationship with him, I saw the nurturing and sensitive side of a man, and I learned to trust men. I took this view into my professional world and allowed the coaching and guidance of male colleagues and leaders into my life.

As a woman who did not have a relationship with my father and was raised by a single mother, my godfather was instrumental in helping me learn to trust men. When a father figure is not present in a child's life, I believe it is important for single mothers to include very carefully vetted, positive male interaction in their children's lives in some capacity. It could be through another trusted family member, a member of your church community, the soccer team coach, Boys & Girls Clubs of America or a godparent like in my case. This will help them understand what to expect of men, show them how men can be, and to help them build trusting relationships with them that will be instrumental for their future as adults. Having a healthy, positive, strong male role model is important for both boys and girls.

Dominating in a male-dominated industry does not mean disdaining masculine energy — in fact, that is counterproductive. Men have a lot of strengths and a lot to teach. For many years in my career, I only had successful male mentors and I learned a lot from them. They taught me how to be aggressive and be swift in getting things done. Now I'm able to use the tools my male mentors have taught me along with my innate natural abilities as a woman to be powerful at every table and in every circle.

As a woman who is in many inner circles and decision-making forums, I take responsibility to bring more women into those environments. My character and conduct will be used to judge other women who look like me and I don't take that responsibility lightly. I want to shape the view that the mainstream has of black women by being an intelligent, hardworking, value-driven, and results-oriented black woman at the table. I advocate for more women at the table by being an impeccable example of female value. This also affords me the right to have an opinion about who is next, and I make it a point to include female representation in the network and pool of candidates to consider for opportunities.

WHY CORPORATE AMERICA NEEDS MORE WOMEN

For the sake of corporate America, and for everyone employed by corporations, there needs to be an increase in female talent at all levels — from entry-level to senior leadership. Women have a proven track record to increase revenue, develop more innovative products, and increase productivity levels in an organization. However, we are still underrepresented, and corporate America and our economy are not benefiting from our highest value. As per the *Catalyst, Pyramid: Women in S&P 500 Companies* statistics[7], women only represent:

- 4.8% of CEOs
- 11.0% of top earners
- 21.2% of board seats
- 26.5% of executive/senior-level officials and managers
- 36.9% of first/mid-level officials and managers
- 44.7% of total employees

According to Morgan Stanley Capital International, an independent provider of research-driven insights and tools for institutional investors, there is a tipping point for peak performance. Its research indicates that having at least three women on a corporate board of directors' team is the point that increases financial performance of a company.[8] Their findings found that in 2015, companies with three more women on their board experienced a Return on Equity of 10.1 percent per year. On the other hand, companies without the same female representation on their boards only achieved an average of 7.4 percent Return

7 https://www.catalyst.org/knowledge/women-sp-500-companies
8 https://www.msci.com/www/blog-posts/the-tipping-point-women-on/0538249725

on Equity.

In other words, bringing more women to the table is not just a diversity conversation, but it is also a discussion about the performance of corporations. This begs the question, *why are corporations still under-recruiting and underutilizing one of its greatest potential and high-value assets?*

For years, women have been working hard for the greater good of others, and not just themselves. A woman who embodies this way of being is the legendary American businesswoman Madam C. J. Walker who has been famously quoted saying, "I am not satisfied in making money for myself. I endeavor to provide employment for hundreds of women of my race." Her accomplishments and journey are indicative of a woman who lived to empower and spread abundance to those around her.

Madam Walker began her life as Sarah Breedlove. She was born to sharecroppers in Louisiana. Her parents and older siblings were slaves. She escaped slavery herself as she was born in 1867, two years after the Thirteenth Amendment had been ratified in the United States and slavery was abolished. She lost her parents to illness and became an orphan at the young age of 6. Her sister and her sister's husband took her in to live with them, but she was mistreated and violated in their home by her brother-in-law. At the age of 14, she got married and was finally able to remove herself from the abusive relationship with her brother-in-law. She had her only child, Leila, with her husband and she became determined to provide her daughter with a formal education, something that she did not get. When her husband passed away and she became a widow at the age of 21, she took her daughter to St. Louis and began working for her brothers, who were successful barbers, to save money to send her daughter to school.

It was when she moved to St. Louis that Sarah Breedlove's life started to change. She was learning how to cut and style hair, as well as how to run a successful business. It was at this time that she also began to lose her own hair. This was not uncommon for those times. A combination of poor diet, harsh lye (a common ingredient in hair soaps at the time), and a lack of indoor plumbing that limited hygiene practices were all factors in causing many people to lose their hair. Sarah used her circumstances to create cosmetic creams and other hair products to relieve her condition.

Sarah had excellent and intuitive leadership skills. When she married Charles Joseph Walker, a newspaper advertising salesman, in 1906, and became Madam C. J. Walker, she combined her unique marketing concepts with his marketing expertise. It was at this point that her business started to grow exponentially. The family moved to Pittsburgh, Pennsylvania in 1908 and opened the Leila College to train "Walker Agents" to use and sell Madam Walker's products.

In 1910, they relocated again to Indianapolis, Indiana, where her client base exploded, and her sales staff grew to almost 1,000 agents all over the United States, Cuba, Costa Rica, Panama, Jamaica, and Haiti. These agents, all of whom were women, didn't just learn to perfect the art of sales from Madame

Walker. The women were also coached on the ideals of women's independence and they were taught the business skills and acumen they would need to become sales agents themselves. When Madam Walker passed away in 1919 at the age of 51, her life's accomplishments included not only becoming an extremely successful businesswoman, but an outspoken and impactful community activist. She joined the leaders of the NAACP in their campaign to create legislation that would make lynching a federal crime, she was a patron of the arts, and a very generous philanthropist making large donations to underfunded black schools and other organizations including the YMCA.

Madam C. J. Walker was not only the first black female millionaire in the United States, but she was also the country's very first self-made female millionaire. Her story is remarkable not only because she overcame challenging life circumstances and became very successful, but her success transcended her. By building an empire, she was able to employ thousands of women in multiple countries and support them in caring for their families. In addition to saving enough money to send her own child to school, she was able to help thousands of women do the same for their children. She used her platform, brand, and money to support community causes that helped people live a better life. Madame C. J. Walker is an example of the power and effect of women when we have an opportunity to be a leader and decision-maker. This is the kind of impact that is missing in corporate America when women are underrepresented.

WHY LEARNING FROM MEN IS IMPORTANT

It is important for women to have both male and female mentors. You will shortchange yourself if you have disdain for the masculine model because men have a lot to teach us. They have been in the professional workplace a lot longer and have been at the helm leading and building for a very long time. As evidenced in the numbers, they also outnumber women in business, leadership roles, and many industries. From a simple supply-and-demand perspective, there are more male mentors available than women. Thus, taking advantage of knowledge available will also mean that we women must learn from men as well.

Whether you are learning from men or women, keep your femininity and assign it its true value. Know that, as a woman, you bring a unique perspective to the problems at hand and the approach to solution designing for those issues. You bring a different strength to the table that only you can bring. Perhaps it is still a man's world today, but that does not mean you cannot play or work in that world and learn as much as possible from it. Become a better version of yourself and knock down the doors in front of you to increase opportunities for yourself and other women who will come after you.

JOIN THE "GIRLS' CLUB"

While I have been blessed with a strong network of males, I have been blessed tenfold with a powerful network of female mentors, colleagues, and friends. I have acquired the friendships of some of the most powerful and dynamic women on Earth. Many of these women have been my trusted allies for over 30 years. In addition to my group of lifelong friends, whom I call my "sister friends," I have also encountered a plethora of dynamic women in the form of clients, vendors, professional peers, and bosses. Lita Cunningham is an example of a female relationship born out of a managerial relationship.

Lita was the senior vice president of Human Resources at Time Inc. and hired me to join a coalition of diversified talent programs implemented within the company. She worked tirelessly to support and guide the new hires in successfully climatizing to the culture of the company and implemented innovative ways to help retain diverse talent. It was really refreshing to work for and with a company that was actively seeking inclusion and working aggressively to open positions for diverse candidates that provided a developmental path to senior roles at the company. After two years of working with Lita, even 16 years later, she remains a trusted confidante and friend whom I love dearly. I have worked with some of the most talented women, like Mitzi Miller, who have gone on to achieve tremendous success.

Mitzi is a friend who I met during her internship at Honey magazine. After meeting her at the office holiday party, I knew instantly she would be a mainstay in my life. Nineteen years later, she has reached success as a published author of several novels, her stories are incredible and some of them have been turned into movies, and television shows. She has even held editor in chief positions at both Jet and Ebony magazines. Mitzi and Lita are just two examples of extraordinary women I have met and became friends with. There is so much that I could say about the women I have developed relationships with along the way who are now powerhouses in their own rights. Powerful networks allow us to influence decisions and direction across industries.

The premise of the "girls' club" is for us women to live life with a capital "E" and that "E" stands for empowerment. This concept is borrowed from the circle of support from men that is known as the "guy code."

The guy code is a dynamic among men in which they support each other. This means that men can battle each other during the workday in the boardroom on opposite sides of the negotiation table, and then go out in the evening for a casual conversation over beer. One guy can buy a new car, and when his buddy buys the same one, he takes it as a compliment. Two guys can be attracted to the same woman and have a gentlemen's agreement that the best man shall win and be content with whoever she decides that she likes. I don't believe that the same can be said overall about women.

I believe that, in general terms, women approach life from the perspective of scarcity, and this dissuades us from empowering and supporting each other as much as we can and should. We live in a world where it can often feel like we are in a game of survival of the fittest. Since the opportunities afforded to women are more limited than what men are offered, it is possible that many women feel that they need to hold onto opportunities for themselves. If we all operated from the mentality of true abundance then we wouldn't feel as territorial, fearful, or threatened by each other. To achieve our highest potential, women need a girls' club — a space where we aren't threatened or feel any negative emotion about each other's success, and champion each other's fulfillment as much as we do our own. We need to support each other so that we can evolve into our own greatest happiness. When each of us embrace abundance, we will naturally create a world where we can all be winners.

There are so many men who are winning because they seem to have figured out the empowerment equation well. They help each other, they do business together, they collaborate even if they don't personally like each other or get along, and they share with each other. Women, on the other hand, tend to be shy about sharing information, don't often go out of their way to enable or create opportunities for each other, and aren't all actively working to advance one another. Perhaps this is because we intrinsically feel that opportunities are scarce, and they are more limited for women according to the data, but if nothing changes then…well, nothing changes.

For the betterment of our entire community, all women need to contribute toward building and sustaining the girls' club. If we all do our part to extend the olive branch to help forward one another, we can create a global impact and change together. Far too often, a small group of women become the only ones to make it. This needs to change. There is power in numbers and we are stronger together than we would ever be as individuals. A woman who helps other women is also helping herself by closing the multiple gender gaps that exist in the corporate world, education, wealth, and much more.

Participating in the girls' club can be as simple as cheering each other on in our individual quests for success, buying a woman's new book or other product, or even attending a fellow sister's event. In today's digital world, it could even be clicking the like button or positively commenting on other women's social media posts. The bottom line is, there is power in numbers and we need to support each other. Join the girls' club and encourage your sisters to do the same.

A strong girls' club is like an expansive Rolodex of "sister friends" that you can count on for support, guidance, and empowerment. Not everyone in your club needs to be your best friend, or even a friend for that matter, but the spirit of your relationship with them should be one of mutual advancement. My girls' club is expansive. I know hundreds of wonderful women and, even though I haven't connected with some of them in years, we continue to show up for each other and celebrate each other's successes. A win for one is a win for all of us in my circle.

To have the privilege of having such a strong network of women around me, I had to be a friend to have a friend. The relationships need to extend two ways and must be mutually beneficial. Be a member of the club by being of service to others and extending yourself to your fellow sisters. The gesture will come back to you. In addition, the more you connect, the more we will all connect, and the more expansive our global girls' club can become.

The female experience is unique and vastly different from the male experience, both personally and professionally. Having an arsenal of knowledgeable and talented women to help you navigate any situation you encounter is a huge benefit. Not every decision in your life will require input or support from another person but knowing who to contact when and for what is a key asset to getting to where you want to be in life. Having access to a network of dynamic and diverse women will provide you with the tools you need to seek the answers you are looking for.

The girls' club is for all of us and we all have a responsibility to build it up. You can start by being the support that you are looking for in other women. Extend yourself and proactively engage other women. Lateral networking is just as important as helping those coming up behind you and reaching out to those ahead of you. Having peer contacts are the building blocks to having influential relationships as a senior leader. The more people you help in your career today, the more people there will be to help you during your time of need. Celebrate a woman today — any woman. Go show some love and spread the message of empowerment. I promise, it will come back to you.

PITTMAN'S RULES:

1. Don't allow subjective roles and norms to dictate how you act or who you can be.
2. Leading in a male-dominated industry does not mean disdaining masculine energy.
3. Your character and conduct will be used to judge other women, so don't take that responsibility lightly.
4. Join the "girls' club" or, if there isn't one around you, start one.
5. Show love to your fellow sisters and spread the message of empowerment.
6. Be a friend to have a friend.

Chapter 9:
FULFILLMENT, MONEY AND ADVENTURE

Living life to the fullest means having the life you want in every aspect of it. This includes your love life, your health and wellness, your social life, your career, experiences and adventures, and much more. It took me years to realize that my career would be there even if I took the time to focus on other areas that are also important to me. Now I keep myself accountable for making me a priority. I encourage you to not just be alive, but to live.

Living life to the fullest is about more than just getting through the day. It is about thriving. Being alive and having functioning vitals should not be confused for living. To live is to flourish and grow. At the start of each day, I ask myself an intentional question: *do I want to just make it through the day or do I want to make the day really count by growing and stretching myself in new ways?* My answer to this question shapes my actions from sunrise to sunset. It sets the tone for my day.

There are days when I decide that I just want to make it through and I have limited inspiration during those times. I just want to exist on those days, but I do so only to recharge and be ready for the rest of the week. It is healthy to have off days when you are not totally on. Megastar Beyoncé Knowles has talked about the importance of having rest. She takes time off to rejuvenate, which ultimately allows her to tap into the inspiration she needs to create her art. Having a day of rest is encouraged in many religions, including Judaism and Christianity. Many Christians set aside Sundays for observance of religion and as a day of rest, and many individuals of the Jewish faith have Sabbath, a dedicated time to rest, from Friday evening to

Saturday evening every week.

Days of rest are a chance to refocus, recalibrate, and recommit to our goals and desires. What is key is that you do not let these less inspirational days become a norm or a habitual part of your life. Allowing too much downtime could become a bad habit that is difficult to break out of. There have been many occasions in the last several years when I have taken too many days off. I have my good days and my bad days. Sometimes I wake up super early and still feel very energized, happy, and inspired to conquer the world. Other times, I don't want to get out of bed. The thought of tackling my day is just too much to bear because I feel like the weight of the world is on my shoulders. Due to burnout, overstress, and overextending myself, I needed longer periods of time to rest.

Constantly being on the go took a toll on my mind, body, and spirit and I needed to just be. Pushing yourself, on days when you need time off, only causes you to require a longer break. On the days when I feel low and have little motivation to take on the tasks on my to-do list, I pause. These moments of pausing and just being have given me the silence I need to quiet my mind. Through silence, I've gained clarity and discovered new truths about who I am.

I've learned that working myself tirelessly will not serve me in the long run. I have been giving 200 percent of myself for someone else's vision for decades. Now looking back, it is hard to believe that I allowed myself to do that for as long as I did. You will never be as valuable to someone else as you are to yourself. When an employer feels that they have no need for you anymore, they will dispose of you and continue with their journey, regardless of how much you have given to them. I have now learned the importance of protecting some of my time and energy for myself and for connections to family, friends, and intimate relationships. Remember to do you and focus a considerable amount of your time on your passion, purpose, and vision for your life.

If you do not know what your passion, purpose, and life vision are, take some time to discover these things. Being as much of your full and whole self, as much as possible, should be your goal for the time that you have on this Earth. Burning yourself out does you, and everyone around you, a disservice. Killing yourself to live up to someone else's dream is not a smart investment. Take the time you need, when you need it, and be responsible to your priorities so that you are not negligent in "adulting." At the same time, make sure that you have enough space in your life to reboot, recharge, and reset.

Like any habit, there is a choice in the matter — you can either choose to continue the pattern or you can break it. Even when I've taken a lot of time to rest, I still have the choice each day to lean in and reset if I choose to do so. Each day is a new opportunity to shift, evolve, and become a better version of yourself. No judgment, no resentment, just acceptance that you are human.

You are not perfect, but the choice to change is available and is always yours to make. Repeatedly, you get to choose to be a better version of yourself in each moment. Fill in the blank for yourself for the following sentence:

I would best serve myself in this moment if I:

____

____

____

As the person, who knows you best, you get to craft your vision.

For me, the answer varies from week to week, day to day, and moment to moment. It ranges from *if I went for a walk, read a chapter from a book about personal finance, did research on the new business I am looking to start, or finished the manuscript of my personal story.* Trust yourself to have the right answer for what you need and lean into each moment of life with excitement and self-assurance. It may require work to live life to the fullest at times. You may have to wake up earlier to hit the gym, stay up a little later to finish a project or grab a nightcap with some girlfriends, but the result will be worth it. The goal is to work toward being the best version of yourself while taking life as it comes with as little resentment, stress, and judgment as possible.

It is about looking back at the end of the road and loving the journey that got you there. It is about watching the movie reel of your life and loving every scene in it. There is a famous Latin proverb that is translated as, "Fortune favors the bold." At its core, it is a reference to the fruit of the labor and the victory you feel after the challenges of the battle have been overcome. The reality is, life has a way of showing up for you in the most magical ways if you dare to live in three-dimensional color.

One of the mottos that I live my life by is to "live life out loud," just as my grandmother did. For the better part of my adulthood, I hid so much of who I was. I limited my self-expression and held back in fully showcasing all of me. From my humor to how I dressed, I was calculated and meticulous. I stood on the sidelines and watched in awe when I saw individuals who were unapologetically themselves. I often hit "like" on social media posts where people were unabashedly themselves, but I failed to express myself in the same way. Influencers like Cardi B truly impress me by how much they allow all of who they are to be shown to the world. Cardi B makes no apologies about who she is, and she expects the world to embrace it, and they do. It is refreshing to experience her because she does not hide any part of who she is. For many years, I saw authentic self-expression as a risk. I hesitated to put myself on the line. On vacations, I stopped myself from jet skiing because I couldn't swim, instead of just putting on the life jacket and trusting that I'd stay afloat. I wasn't living my life in full color for fear of failing or being judged.

Growing up in New York, self-preservation was vital to surviving. My experiences growing up hardwired me to constantly assess for risks in any situation and proceed with caution always. It took the death of my grandmother to see that I wasn't living life out loud and was missing out on truly living. My life was good, but my life wasn't great. When my grandmother passed away, she knew, as well as everyone around her, that she would not have changed a single moment of her life. She was who she wanted to be, and she lived life with no regrets. In her, I saw what I should be, which was a woman who did not hold back, and for me, that was a beautiful thing.

Today, living life out loud is exactly what I'm doing. Penning my first manuscript, and becoming an author, is an ode to my grandmother and a symbol of fully expressing who I am. I am no longer holding back. In the past, I was too afraid to admit that I had a story to tell. I felt like I was not qualified to share my truth. I didn't think that anybody would want to hear me, Ericka Pittman, of all people. I have finally woken up. I am finally ready to share my truth and share all of who I am with the world. To give myself to the world, I need to ensure that I take care of my needs in all areas of life, and that is exactly what I am doing now.

My needs shift as my life shifts. I prioritize my needs based on what is currently happening and what external factors are impacting me. I commit to doing it all, while knowing that I don't have to do everything all at the same time. If there's a lot going on in my professional life, I intentionally focus on my career at the expense of putting limited effort and time into other areas. I am always mindful of what I'm neglecting so that I can focus on those aspects at another time. I take each day as it comes. Each day, I assess what I need to do to achieve my best self that day. And with deep breathing, meditation, reflection, and prayer I set my intentions. The key is to be in tune with what your mind, body, and spirit needs and to take the appropriate actions to fulfill them.

Tapping into yourself, and truly understanding what's overflowing and what's lacking for you, is the only way to make the appropriate adjustments in your life. Sometimes we get greedy, lazy, or simply choose to be ignorant. For instance, you may be gaining a lot of momentum at work, so you keep pushing yourself in that area. You continue to put in the long hours, weekends get occupied tending to work priorities, there's heavy travel flying between offices, and then BAM — you fall sick with a cold because your immune system is compromised due to a poor diet, limited sleep, and just sheer exhaustion. Or perhaps you meet a great guy, but the relationship doesn't go anywhere after the first date because you are always busy and can't make the time to meet him again. The relationship dissipates because you haven't held up your end of the bargain and nurtured it enough to create a solid foundation with him. Getting what you want in each aspect of your life will require you to act on each aspect of your life. There is no secret sauce to work-life balance. Work-life integration is the result of the decisions that you make, and the areas in your life that you decide to spend time on. Most importantly, work-life balance is contingent upon your ability to pivot.

Ask yourself, how quickly do I shift gears to focus on the life priority at hand?

The key to succeeding in all areas of your life is YOU. You must consistently check in with yourself and evaluate where your needs and priorities are at that moment. You can then adjust your actions to support and feed the areas that are lacking. When you operate this way, and constantly work to adjust and nurture all your needs, you will lead a well-balanced life in every way possible. By doing so, at the end of it all, you should be able to say with confidence that you lived a full life. The various individual parts of your life are collectively like an orchestra and your goal should be to make it sound like a symphony. Each sound has its place and they should harmoniously play together. My music sheet is my calendar.

I put everything in my digital calendar. I love it for so many reasons. It helps me visualize how I'm allocating my time and where I am allocating it. It allows me to plan, and I can create lead times that function as reminders. In this way, everything that needs to stay top of mind does stay top of mind. While my work life and personal life have very different commitments and schedules, I prefer to combine them into one central calendar where I can track both parts of my life. This is one way that I tune into whether I am neglecting either my career or my personal commitments. It also helps create time synergies that assist me in optimally using my time. Being effective in how you spend the hours in a day also requires being protective of it. It can become so easy to overspend your time in any one area. Have you ever sat down to watch an episode of your favorite TV show, but end up watching five episodes back to back? Do you ever get started on a work assignment and get so engrossed in it that you don't even realize the lunch hour has come and gone? Set hard stops for yourself and know when to move on to the next thing.

I have a philosophy that the things you are putting off are the very things that you need to do right now. Being able to see on my calendar how I'm allocating my time also serves as a reminder that I do have the time to do the very thing that I've been putting off, or that I can shift other things to make time for what I am putting off. It could be having a 10-minute phone call to deliver bad news to someone, getting in a 30-minute workout at home, or doing meal preparation for the week — I find myself using the excuse of not having enough time as justification to not do it. My calendar shows me that there is always time, it simply requires that I be intentional about how I spend it. While I didn't operate in this way at the start of my career, I did ultimately learn that I can have it all, just not all at the same time.

It is a myth that you must put your personal life on the back burner to have a very successful career. Yes, you must prioritize your various needs and commitments, yes you must make some sacrifices, and yes, sometimes you will have to say no to things that you really want to say yes to. But that in no way needs to preclude you from engaging in a healthy personal life. I have made significant gains over the years in my professional life, but I still have a very full personal life that I love.

I am very social, and I go out often. I have an amazing group of girlfriends, and I meet so many fantastic men and women regularly. I travel, shop, read, work out, eat well, pray, and date. This does not mean that I can always do everything I want to do when I want to do it. I make compromises, sacrifices, and decisions all the time. And that's okay because I know that I can't always do what I want to do at the expense of doing what I need to do. When you have a clear understanding of what your definition of success is and what you want your personal life to be like, you can manage your schedule to achieve all the things you want in your life, though it may not necessarily be when you want it. You have 24 hours in a day. You must decide what you're going to do with them.

DO BUSINESS BEFORE PLEASURE

Growing up, my mother would always tell me, "Do your homework on Friday!" This explains a larger, but simple, state of being which is to get ahead by getting the hard stuff out of the way first.

My mother was a big believer in rituals. She would do her nails on Sundays. Meal preparation would be done on both Saturdays and Tuesdays for the whole week. She always headed out to do grocery shopping on Fridays and would get a glazed donut for me and ice cream for herself on our way back from the store. She ran a well-oiled machine and that is one of the many reasons why she was able to have a successful career while being a single mother who gave her daughter everything that she needed.

My mother used to always encourage, or rather enforce, that I pull out my homework after we got home from grocery shopping to finish all my school assignments before the weekend even started. I hated that she used to make me do this. I was often annoyed at her for it and was vocal about it. I had to stay up Friday nights to do homework even though all I wanted to do was play with my dolls or watch movies. I realize now that doing my homework on Fridays was never about the homework. My mother was preparing me for the larger deliverables that were to come in my life. She was teaching me the importance of doing business before pleasure. This is a lesson that I still think about to this day, even though I'm still working on regularly implementing it in my life.

I am a procrastinator by nature; it is part of my personality. I often resist and wrestle with the very lesson my mother taught me about doing business before pleasure. Often, I push off complicated, confusing, or intense tasks. I convince myself that I need to be "ready" to tackle them or that I need to be in the "mood" to do it. As such, I wait and wait and wait until I finally have no choice but to get it done, or it's too late to do anything about it. While my mother's lesson was to do the things that need to be done regardless of how I felt about doing it, I often wait until I am emotionally ready to tackle what I need to. I am constantly working on getting out of my emotions and my thoughts to complete business tasks first so that I can enjoy the pleasures of my life without stress. It is only through specific and intentional discipline daily that I am now overcoming my natural inclination to push things off.

Sometimes I get it right though. I have Saturdays when you can find me working out first thing in the morning, then tackling my work to-do list and errands before going out for a day of fun and pleasure. Even on my 42nd birthday in 2018, I took the day off to lounge in a cabana by the pool, sipping Champagne with my girlfriends. In between drinks, I took an hour to work on this very manuscript. Making time for business, even during pleasure, has grounded me and kept me on track to achieve my goals and dreams. Regularly making to-do lists, and prioritizing items on my list in order of urgency and impact on my overall goals, is also helping me form the habit of tackling things regardless of how I feel. When I find myself distracted or getting off track with my plan, I revisit my to-do list to refocus and re-energize myself.

I have some ways to go before I apply my mother's lesson all the time, but I have seen the positive results when I do follow her words of advice. I apply this lesson to money management as well — necessities first, investments second, and indulgences last. I expend the resources to treat myself, but I do so knowing that there is a place and time for it in my life.

PERSONAL FINANCE 101

As many times as I have learned about compound interest, I never really maximized on the principles of it in my early 20s. Saving and investing as early as possible is so important to your bottom line, or in other words, the size of your bank account. Personal finance is an area of your life that you must learn to master because you will always need it. You need money to survive but you need CREDIT to truly live, and therefore, you will always need to manage your money accordingly.

Managing your money is about more than just earning an income and spending it to live. It is about learning to budget, optimizing on your taxes, saving, and most importantly, investing. My biggest money mistake is not investing enough in the early years of my career. I wish I educated myself sooner, invested more in Index funds, and benefited from compound interest and dividends for a longer period. The truth is, I used to be afraid of investing. It was outside my comfort zone because I had limited knowledge about it. I didn't know what it was or how best to navigate it. My family didn't have wealth. My mother had just enough to provide for our needs and she spent whatever little she had extra on giving me great experiences. There wasn't much left to invest so she didn't know a lot about it and, therefore, wasn't able to teach me about it.

Not having someone that I trusted to teach me about investing, or to guide me in making these financial decisions, impacted my financial activities, or the lack thereof. My risk appetite was low, my knowledge in personal finance was limited, and I didn't have the gumption to go figure out the complicated world of investments on my own. I did all the things that I saw my mother, grandmother, and aunt do growing up. I saved. I stuffed money under the mattress and put some of it in traditional, low return mutual funds at the bank. I planned for retirement by maximizing my 401(k), and I got life insurance. I made down payments, got mortgages, and purchased investment properties. I did all the things that I was told to do, but I didn't begin to learn the art of investing until just recently.

As I moved into different roles in my career and was in positions where I had to navigate large acquisitions and merger deals, I gained knowledge about the world of investing and how to make money make you more money. I am more comfortable when making investment decisions. Knowing what I know now, and understanding how important money management is, I would likely have majored in finance in college. I would have put money toward investing in the stock market instead of making purchases on the latest trends and excursions, though those experiences were great! They were fun but the penny you invest today begets a dollar tomorrow — if you do it right.

Unfortunately, I didn't know to correct my money management woes because I genuinely believed, at that time, that I was being financially prudent. I thought I was checking all the boxes for financial requirements, and I suppose I was if my only intention was to have enough financial support to retire meagerly at age 68. However, to achieve financial freedom long before retirement, there are some fundamental investment principles that must be applied. The key is to start as early as possible. I am just learning the fundamentals and, if I knew then what I know now, I would be so close to already being financially free. Read a few books, take a few classes, and ask a few questions to build your knowledge to make educated decisions. Here are five money hacks to start you off:

1. **Cash is king,** and it is also a strong indicator of what you should or shouldn't do. If you can't afford to pay cash for it, then you shouldn't buy it. Of course, this rule does not apply to good debt, which is any purchase that will help you

build equity and assets. Getting a mortgage to buy a home, for example, is an equity-producing purchase. Most people don't have a few hundred-thousand dollars readily available to make a big purchase, and a loan from a bank is necessary in these cases. On the other hand, taking trips on credit, going out to restaurants and concerts on borrowed funds, or shopping with your credit card will not serve you well. Credit in all those cases creates a false sense of security. You are tricked into believing that you have the money that you don't have; therefore, you make purchases that you shouldn't be making.

2. **Credit is queen** because it is necessary to becoming financially free in the long term. Not all money is created the same. Some money is more expensive than other money, meaning that depending on your credit score, it may cost you a lot more to pay back borrowed money. The percentage of fees for borrowing money from a creditor is interest, and the amount you pay is influenced by a variety of factors, including your credit score. It is a reverse co-relation. If your credit score is high, then the interest rates you get charged will generally be lower. On the other hand, if your credit score is bad, or low, then the interest rate you get charged will generally be high. It may be tempting to use your credit on nice-to-haves but know that your purchase may actually cost you significantly more in the long run of paying it off, factoring in your interest rates. For example, that dope pair of $1,200 boots that you had to charge on credit and pay over time may end up costing you more than $2,000 by the time to pay down the monthly payments. Credit cards

should be used for the things you need instead of the things you want. Your credit history is your responsibility and it is up to you to protect it. You will always need your credit in life and, being responsible with it, will serve you in the long run.

3. **Look for less and be a smart shopper.** I don't know about you, but I'm all about getting a good deal. I have a general rule of thumb, which is to avoid paying full price as much as possible. With the surge of e-commerce, it is easier than ever before to shop and compare prices all from the comfort of your home. I also look for coupons online and use them when possible. Get into the habit of buying in bulk so that you can avoid paying extra convenience fees. Buying a dozen paper hand towels from a club store and storing them in your home will cost you way less than going to your local corner store to buy hand towels one roll at a time. And bonus, it will save you time as well!

4. **Reward yourself with rewards when possible.** Reward programs are great, and I sign up for many to get access to additional savings, free gifts and prizes, and other perks. You can take this a step further and link your reward program accounts. Credit cards, hotel rewards programs, and airline rewards programs are best maximized when they are all linked together. I once took my mom on a six-day adventure to Hawaii all paid for through reward points. I used the perks from various programs to purchase our plane tickets, accommodations, rental car, and I even used vouchers for discounts on meals at the hotel. Points can create tremendous savings and let you treat yourself without having to dip into your savings — or worse, charging items on your credit

card.

5. **Meal prep your way to savings.** Yes, that's correct. Preparing your meals and eating at home is one of the surest ways to save a ton of money. It may seem insignificant on the surface, but it is a lifestyle change that can be very impactful on your wallet and health. The average person, depending on the city you live in, could spend $20 to $30 a day on food if they buy their morning coffee, breakfast, and lunch. If you do that five days a week, that equals $100 to $150 a week! What seems like a small amount of money each day amounts to thousands of dollars for the entire year. Do yourself a favor. Make time for preparing your meals in your weekly schedule, pay a visit to the local grocery store, and cook your meals. This isn't just good practice for your bank account, but your waistline will also thank you in the long run.

At its core, personal finance is really about what you want for your life in the long term. It is easy to make short-term decisions for instant gratification, but you owe it to yourself to think about how those actions will impact the larger vision you have for your life (this advice applies to all areas of your life). Don't be tempted by anything you see on social media, your social circles, or entertainment. You cannot judge the full landscape of someone's financial portfolio just by seeing what they wear, what they drive, and where they live. Someone may appear to be doing well or doing all the right things, but they may not be maximizing their income to the fullest. I used to be this kind of person — I was a great saver but a poor investor.

And then there are others who may be great investors, but they spend everything they earn on an expensive lifestyle. Personal finance is different for every individual. The key is to prioritize what is important to you based on your long-term goals, create a plan that supports them, and have the discipline to achieve your vision.

LIFE IS SHORT, SO GO ON THE ADVENTURE

I encourage everyone to travel. Experience new places and expose yourself to new people and cultures. You don't have to be a hero at the office and forgo vacation days to work. Everyone needs a break to recharge, and traveling will help you evolve as a person. Adventure and new experiences are important for both your personal and professional lives.

Travel is pivotal to the process of growth. Exploring environments outside of your own is a great way to expand your perspective, humility, and empathy for others. Exposing yourself to new people, diverse cuisines, fresh locales, and new social dynamics will help you become more aware of the global market and society we live in, and help you understand your place in it. Knowing that you play a tiny role on this planet will help you develop greater compassion and appreciation for the world around you. Familiarity breeds contempt and that is not supportive of growth and evolution. When you travel you get to experience the new, the unfamiliar, the unexpected. You learn to let go because there's so much beyond you, and you gain a new respect for life.

Through my own personal globe-trotting adventures, one of my greatest learnings has been that, as much as people seem to be different, we are all the same. Human nature is just human nature. We all have the same basic needs. We all feel happiness, sadness, fear, and excitement. We all experience heartbreak, love, connection, friendship, and loss. We are all trying to figure out this thing called life, but we each do it in our own way. Everyone is searching for love, peace, and happiness. Some of us get there faster than others, and some of us never get there. The clearer we are about the power each of us holds, and how much we all want the same thing, the more harmoniously we can all live together. Travel has helped me understand my place in the grander realm of the world.

By seeing the world and all its grandeur, I have learned that who I am is more powerful than who I thought I was growing up as a girl in East New York, Brooklyn. I matter and my contributions matter at a global scale. I became a more compassionate person to those around me and I became more compassionate toward myself. I didn't feel alone in the world anymore. My first international trip was to Germany when I was 20 years old. I was committed to experiencing Europe for my 21st birthday. I flew out of New York's largest airport, the John F. Kennedy international airport, alone. I planned to visit a friend in Germany who would then accompany me to France. In my own frenzy, I booked my flight to the wrong airport in Germany and ended up hours away from where I needed to be.

Once I landed in Germany, my mind shifted to panic. I was terrified. I was in a foreign country and the only German words I knew were *danke* (meaning thanks), *ja* (meaning yes), and *nein* (meaning no). The little German I knew could not even be strung together to make a full sentence. I had no choice but to lean on those around me, who were all strangers. I stopped people, asked them questions, and asked for advice on how I could go from Dusseldorf to Kaiserslautern in Germany. Everyone I spoke to was so nice, so helpful, and so accommodating; they were patient with me and were all willing to help me on my journey. Through the support of strangers (and God almighty), I got to my destination safely. When I returned home to the United States after my European adventure, I had a different perspective of my role in the world and all the ways, big or small, to help others on their journey. The simple and random acts of kindness and compassion I experienced on the other side of the world opened up my mind to the person I needed to become in my own life. I understood the value of service through this adventure and I became committed to helping others.

Later, my early years of consistent personal travel were combined with professional travel. I was required to travel solo around the world when I sold advertising.

One of my categories was travel and it was my job to go to different destinations/countries to conduct sales pitches. On behalf of the publication I represented, I would pitch to each country's tourism board and local vendors to purchase advertising. All the alone time that I got by traveling solo helped me learn a lot about myself — my fears, insecurities, and strengths. I was

25 years old when I started globe-trotting alone and learned to adjust to the uncertainty of being in new and unfamiliar places. I am so grateful for the many adventures I have had throughout my life. For me, it started in childhood when my mother would save what she could to take me to new places. In her own way, she was showing me how to expand my wings and seek to learn about the things that were unknown to me. This shifted to fun adventures for me as a young adult traveling with friends, and eventually led to a career that required me to catch many flights. So much of what I have learned about myself and the world stems from the many adventures I have had. You don't know what you don't know, so I highly encourage you to seek unfamiliar places and experiences. Put yourself in situations where you will discover what is currently unknown to you. I promise, you will evolve in ways that you never thought possible.

PITTMAN'S RULES:

1. Have days of rest to refocus, recalibrate, and recommit yourself to living.
2. Live life out loud.
3. You have 24 hours in a day. Decide how you are going to spend it. And don't forget to use a calendar while you are at it.
4. Get ahead by getting the hard stuff out of the way first.
5. Learn to master your personal finance because you will always need it.
6. Travel as much as you can. Experience new places and expose yourself to new people and cultures.

Chapter 10

CONCLUSION

Your life is for living the fully expressed version of yourself. Don't wait to live a fully expressed life because tomorrow is not guaranteed, and the best time is N.O.W. (No Other Way). This is a lesson that I learned later in my life as I reflected on the death of my grandmother. It is important to be great, to work hard, and to do good for others, but never forget that you are on this Earth to live your best life and to share your soul without any inhibitions. Love yourself, love others, and be awakened to the beauty of this world with an open heart. It is through love that we will leave our greatest impact.

To have love for everything just as it is (or isn't), is the most powerful state of being. When you obsess about outcomes in your life that were not what you wanted at the time, romanticize about what might have been, or expend energy to fuel negative thoughts, you are taking away from your own power. This is a manifestation of the "why me" mind-set that comes with victimhood. It masks itself as an effective way to manage stress, but venting is a fleeting positive feeling. It feels good temporarily, but in the long term it will not serve you. The mind-set of "victimhood" will blind you from seeing the beauty of your life, those around you, and even those who aren't around.

I have had an estranged relationship with my father. Its very existence is rooted in its non-existence in my life. I haven't seen my father since I was five years old. He left and never came back. For many years, from my teens to my late-20s, I harbored so many negative feelings toward him. I was angry, frustrated, unforgiving, and felt just about every emotion obverse to that of love. I hated that my father was not accountable in my life or to his role as my parent. It upset me that he abandoned our relationship and didn't give me a choice in the matter. I often thought about what my life would have been like had my father been around. I spent countless hours and far too much energy trying to figure out why he didn't show up for me, why he never came back to me, why he never called me on April 18 each year to wish me happy birthday, why he left in the first place, why, why, why??? I had so many questions, but I didn't have concrete answers for any of them. Sometimes I thought that perhaps I wasn't good enough for him to spend time with, and other times I didn't care what his reasoning was because whatever the root of the problem was, it would never be a good enough excuse. I was hurt and deeply impacted. No matter how I looked at it, nothing made sense to me.

I dwelled on my father abandoning me — lamented even. I judged every relationship I had, from romantic to business alike, from the negative feelings I had for my father. I made all my relationships about the one failed relationship that abruptly ended when I was five. I replayed the pain of not having my father in my life for so long. It wasn't until I finally saw the impact of this way of being that I realized I had to stop. I got tired of being angry and holding him in such a negative place in my heart. It was exhausting, and it was sucking the zest out of my life. This way of being wasn't healthy for me and it wasn't nurturing for those around me. It was impacting my ability to love. It was only when I changed the way I saw my father that my life shifted.

It wasn't until I turned 36 years old that I finally saw my

father in a new light — not as my father, but as a human being in his own right. As a human being, he like the rest of us would make his own mistakes, face the implications of his own decisions, and experience his own feelings. He was a person trying to navigate the waters of life just as I was. I remember thinking, "If I can look past my own mistakes and love myself despite them, then I can look past his mistakes and love him." I didn't have to take responsibility for his actions, but I could take responsibility for my reaction to them. It became clear to me that, while I may never know why my father chose not to be present in my life, his reasons had nothing to do with me. It was never about me to begin with. It was always about him. Once I was able to see my father through love, I was finally able to forgive him and to truly love the life that I had exactly as it was.

I had a mother who raised me all on her own. Would I have been as close to my mother had my father not left? Maybe. Maybe not. The answer no longer mattered because what I had was a strong bond with my mother who is an incredible woman, and I love it exactly as it is. Would I have had to grow up in a low-income neighborhood amid poverty and violence had my father been there to financially support my mother and me? Maybe. Maybe not. This too did not matter because I grew up in a place that made me who I am today — an independent, resourceful, and fearless warrior. I love who I am exactly as I am. While it took me years of self-reflection to come to this realization, I have learned that love is the only path to love. Instead of obsessing over why my father did not take accountability in his relationship with me, I needed to focus on taking accountability for all the relationships in my own life.

Just as I had done years ago, I encourage you to ask yourself *"how am I contributing to the relationships I am in?"* When your mom and dad ask you to come home for dinner on a Saturday night, are you showing up? Are you resentful that you had to miss a night with the girls to hang out with your parents? Or are you bringing joy into your parents' home, and maybe a bottle of wine as well? When you realize that it has been an entire year since you have seen your old college roommate, do you pick up the phone and arrange a plan to get together? Or do you just let it go because it is too much trouble to be the one to plan?

Ask yourself who you are in the relationships in your life and if you are taking accountability for your role in them. Healthy relationships require fostering, attention, thought, energy, and love. Be more mindful of what you are bringing to other people and less about what others are bringing to you, or what you think others should bring to you. For years, my romantic love life had been shaped by what I was focusing on. I had been preoccupied by what I wasn't getting instead of thinking about what I was giving.

I believe in intimate and romantic love. I want to spend the rest of my life with my soul mate and have a family. I envision spending Thanksgiving with my husband and children at my in-law's home, and I envision all of us going to New York to spend Christmas with my family and skating in Central Park. I see exactly what I want. Even though I am so clear on my vision for my future, I have still struggled with love in my life because I had been focusing on the wrong things for years.

I have a very interesting relationship with romantic love. I love very hard. I have given my all to partners in the past, but things did not work out. They did not return to me what I wanted from them. It took me years to recognize that I have an unrealistic expectation of how love is supposed to show up in my life.

I realized that the love I was sharing with others, for the better half of my adult life, was conditional. I only wanted to give my love if it was being returned to me in an equal amount. I wanted the same in return for what I was giving. I also wanted it to feel easy and good even though the love that I was giving was not free-flowing. I created conditions and boundaries to determine how, when, where, and what I would give to others. I only loved those who I believed were deserving of my heart. I only loved kind people. I only trusted people who I loved. I only, I only, I only. I placed so many parameters around who, what and how I chose to love that it confined me to a tiny emotional box. In being this way, I restricted my own ability to give or receive love.

Love is supposed to feel easy, pure, and free-flowing. It is kind, and it is not supposed to come with conditions. To love with expectations is not real love at all. To love another human being is to powerfully connect with them. I have learned that my love doesn't have to be so heavy or restrictive. It can simply be positive energy that I choose to share freely with others. When love flows easily, life will also flow without bumps.

Love is an emotion, and, like all other emotions, every person expresses it in their own way. It is just like other feelings, such as anger, frustration, and sadness — every emotion shows up differently for each person. Love is no different. People express their love in the ways that they know how. While I knew how I loved, I failed to see that others will not show their love in the same way that I do. I express my love through time, energy, and by always showing up. My father failed to show up for me, so I subconsciously translated that to him not loving me. I then took that view into my romantic relationships. If a man did not "show up" for me and give me his time and energy the same way that I did, then I did not see him as loving. I expected the men I dated to equally match the time and energy that I was giving to them. When they didn't meet my expectations, I would shut down and wouldn't be able to see their acts of love for what they were.

I now understand that I had it all wrong for so many years. Love is a selfless emotion. It is supposed to be unconditional. I can love another human being in a way that is genuine to me and they can do the same in return. The way I love is simply a reflection of who I am, and the way someone else loves is an illustration of who they are. Love is not a business commodity and it will not be bought and sold in equal amounts. Love is free. It is not to be bought, sold, or traded. It is supposed to be easy and fluid. Like laughing or breathing, giving love feeds my soul. It nourishes me. Giving love is about me and not about the other person. As selfless as love is, it is also selfish. Much like forgiveness, you give love for yourself and not for the other person.

To give love is to feed your spirit and to create peace within your heart. Give up hope that someone else will love you the same way you love them. Let go of any illusions about what love should look like. Don't get trapped looking for a certain kind of love, because every single human being expresses love in their own unique way. Loving another without expectation is a powerful state of being. It is freedom to create the life you desire for yourself without handing over the control to do so to another person. The power to create the life of your dreams, and live life out loud, rests within you. Once you realize this superpower, you will see just how beautiful the world is around you. You will no longer just see the stars, but you will see them in full 3-D.

I was previously invited to participate in a delegation for the United States in the Middle Eastern country of Qatar. Our mission was to identify financial and investment solutions with the United States' minority population in the country, along with government and private-sector institutions in the region. It was a weeklong immersion trip in the country and an opportunity to learn about the infrastructure and growth opportunities there. The entire experience was incredible from start to finish. On multiple occasions during my time there, I found myself stunned that I had been given a seat at this table to represent my people at a global scale and identify solutions to socio-economic barriers that have plagued our community.

Toward the end of my trip, I woke up early one morning and walked over to the beach by our hotel. I put my feet in the water. I needed to touch the Persian Gulf and feel the ocean. I looked down at my phone and realized that the sun would be rising shortly. Thrilled at the idea of seeing the sun rise so far east in the world, I ran back to my hotel room balcony to take in the view.

The sky was breathtaking. It was pink, like the hue of cotton candy. I had no words to describe how beautiful it was. I tried to take pictures and videos using my phone camera, but it was not the same. There was no camera in the world that could have captured the vibrancy of what my naked eyes saw. I thought, forget the camera, just be present in the beauty of nature. I saw the sun's rays in full three-dimensional color. In that moment, all I could feel was gratitude.

I was thankful and so in love with the life that I had. I was appreciative of all the hard work, sacrifice, and emotions that led me to be given this opportunity. All of it made sense in the moment that I truly saw the colors of the sun as it rose over the Persian Gulf, alone, with no visual confirmation of this experience other than my own eyes. This life that I had was simply meant for me. I realized as I watched the sun rise that I have a responsibility to love my life, the lives around me, and all living things.

One of the proudest moments of my life was being able to take my mother on a trip to Hawaii. My mother had always wanted to experience Hawaii, even as far back as when I was a young girl. She wanted to celebrate her 30th birthday there and started saving up for her trip to do so. However, due to certain life circumstances that occurred, she had to use her savings for other expenses. I still remember the look of sadness on her face when she realized that she could not go to Hawaii to celebrate that monumental birthday. I was about 9 years old at that time, but I knew my mother was disappointed. In that moment, I vowed to one day take her on a trip of a lifetime to experience the wonders of the Aloha State. My opportunity to do so came many years later.

During birthday celebrations that I planned for her 60th birthday, I surprised my mother with the announcement that I would be taking her on an all-expenses paid, luxurious trip to Honolulu. She was shocked and thrilled, sobbing with joy in front of all her guests. I was overcome with happiness to be able to make that dream come true for my mother. She had given me a lifetime of joy, diverse experiences, adventure, and happiness. This was a small gesture of my gratitude to her.

We flew to Hawaii, lounged by the water, shared drinks and delicious meals with each other, meandered along the beach, danced, laughed together, and bonded in an incredible and new way. My mother and I were always very close, but this trip gave us an opportunity to be even more open with each other. We shared and talked about things that we had never spoken of previously. It was the best experience for both of us. It was during this adventure that I realized that she was, and had always been, my best friend. I understood that love has no bounds. Even though I loved my mother so much, I have grown to love her even more with time. Love always keeps on giving and expanding.

Don't be afraid to share love no matter what experiences

you have had in the past. Allow yourself to express uninhibited love — unabashed, out loud, and proud. Love is an abundant emotion that will replenish itself repeatedly the more you share and give it. You are what you repeatedly do, so if you always come from a place of love, you will always be full of love. Love what you had in the past, love what is to come, but most importantly, love what you have in the present. N.O.W.

Time is your most precious commodity and, by living in the present, you will find its greatest value. As a young woman, I did not understand that time is finite, and I was taking away from it each time I thought about the past. I was constantly focused on what had already happened, or how my life would have been if I had the things that I wanted. If I were given an opportunity to go back in time and speak to my younger self, I would help young Ericka Pittman understand the gift of time.

How we use our time tremendously impacts the kind of life we create for ourselves. My grandmother understood this more than anyone I have ever known. She was a fearless woman, and through her fearlessness, she became timeless in her own right. She was not confined by the binds of her race and gender during a time when everyone had an opinion about what she could and could not do. She did things her way and on her own terms. She was unbothered by what the past looked like because her priority was the present. Being this way gave her a life and a family that she was proud of. She was always full of happiness and peace.

My grandmother used to always tell me to never let

grass grow under my feet. She was encouraging me to live my life without wasting time thinking about what happened, mourning the past, being fearful, feeling anxious, or having regrets. Understanding this now, I am intentional about living in the present and remaining in the flow of life as it unfolds. By focusing on my life in the moment, I can let go of the past and not allow it to bind me.

The woman I am today is living in harmony. I am aligned with myself and the world around me. While success is still very important to me, it is no longer one of the top priorities in my life. My priorities now are internally focused. I am looking within and continuing to rediscover and re-create myself each day. Life really can be easy, but people make it complicated. By being radically different from who I have been in the past, I am able to create radically different results for my life. You, too, can re-create and rediscover yourself. You have the universe within you and all you need to do is look within. You are your own greatest teacher.

While my story has taken you on a journey about business, money, authenticity, and so much more, I hope that you see that the foundation to living a life you love, is love. The underpinning of your most important work is internal. Focus on yourself and the rest will come. Prioritize healing and learning, and your life will flow in harmony.

So, what are you waiting for? Go, do it now! Start living. And do it out loud! N.O.W.

-NO OTHER WAY..

Love and Light.

PITTMAN'S RULES:

1. The path to love is through love.
2. To love is to be selfless and selfish.
3. Your life is for you. Live it .
4. Time is a rare and precious commodity.
5. Take accountability for the relationships in your life.
6. Express love authentically and allow others to express their love authentically.
7. Live life out loud — in full, three-dimensional color.

RECAP OF PITTMAN'S RULES:

1. Know that everything happens for a reason and you are exactly where you need to be.
2. Trust the process of life. Every moment, opportunity, challenge, and person are necessary for the lessons and blessings that are to come.
3. Seek advice from your early mentors — the women in your family who know you best. Find your tribe and create a community of trusted advisers around you and lean on them for support. You don't have to do it alone.
4. Run your race your own way and on your own time.
5. Explore the unfamiliar. Try new things and expand your life.
6. Roll call your gratitude list.
7. Trust your intuition and allow it to be your guiding compass.
8. You already have everything you need to realize your dreams. Don't wait or hold off on prioritizing their desires tomorrow because someday may never come.
9. Life happens when you are in the game. Act.
10. You don't have to have it all figured out to set goals. Make short-term and immediate goals to get started and immensely focus on them.
11. Calculated risks are the seeds of success. Not taking a chance will keep you right where you are.
12. Make yourself a priority. You will be all the more happy and successful for it.
13. Learn to laugh at yourself, including the things that the world around you says are wrong about you.
14. Don't be afraid to raise your hand and speak.
15. Just because you are from it does not mean that you are of

it.

16. Don't be ashamed of your past circumstances. They have made you who you are today.

17. Don't be so hard on yourself. Learn to master your inner voice.

18. Be vulnerable and let the world see who you really are. Let your personality shine and share your story. People will love you all the more for it.

19. Ask for what you want in life and be unapologetic about it.

20. Always be bigger than your circumstances.

21. Femininity and sexuality are equally powerful but distinctly different. Learn to use each one as it should be used.

22. Be unapologetically feminine. It will make you stand out.

23. Protect your reputation at all costs, otherwise it will cost you.

24. Learn to effectively use the various elements of your feminine energy. You will be all the more successful because of it.

25. Femininity is not a weakness. Do not misinterpret its gentleness for a loss of power.

26. Always have female mentors who can guide you in effectively leveraging your femininity.

27. Do not forget your earliest mentors, the women who have been in your life from the beginning.

28. Harness the power of femininity in your professional and personal lives, including your friendships.

29. Employ the "Michelle Obama effect" in your personal life. Being feminine in your marriage or partnership is not a sign of weakness.

30. Talk about femininity so that we can help all women effectively tap into the power of theirs.

31. "If You Can Dream It, You Can Build It."
32. Be selfish and prioritize yourself.
33. Unapologetically be your authentic self.
34. Actively manage your ambitions.
35. Discover your "why" and keep it simple.
36. Celebrate your own achievements.
37. Approach your future with childlike wonder and embrace it.
38. Ask yourself the question, what can I do now that will put me ahead in the future?
39. Be aware of change, accept it, and embrace it.
40. Have a strategy, not a plan.
41. "Man, you was who you was 'fore you got here" ~ JAY-Z
42. "It takes a village to raise a child" — take turns being the village and the child.
43. Write your own narrative. Don't wait for others to validate your choices.
44. Take responsibility for the choices you make.
45. Make no concessions and make no excuses. Unapologetically be yourself.
46. Say "yes" to your own needs and desires. Stop making yourself priority number two.
47. Fake it til you make it. Eventually, you will no longer have to fake it.
48. Unreasonable goals require unreasonable staying power and belief in self.
49. Be your biggest advocate. Negotiate. And don't settle.
50. Put your past aside and concentrate on what is to come.
51. All things build on the foundation of integrity.
52. Hard work and perseverance supersede talent.
53. Don't allow subjective roles and norms to dictate how you

act or who you can be.

54. Leading in a male-dominated industry does not mean disdaining masculine energy.

55. Your character and conduct will be used to judge other women, so don't take that responsibility lightly.

56. Join the "girls' club" or, if there isn't one around you, start one.

57. Show love to your fellow sisters and spread the message of empowerment.

58. Have days of rest to refocus, recalibrate, and recommit yourself to living.

59. Live life out loud.

60. You have 24 hours in a day. Decide how you are going to spend it. And don't forget to use a calendar while you are at it.

61. Get ahead by getting the hard stuff out of the way first.

62. Learn to master your personal finances because you will always need it.

63. Travel as much as you can. Experience new places and expose yourself to new people and cultures.

64. The path to love is through love.

65. To love is to be selfless and selfish.

66. Take accountability for the relationships in your life.

67. Express love authentically and allow others to express their love authentically.

68. Live life out loud — in full, three-dimensional color.

AUTHOR BIO

Ericka Pittman is a marketing professional from Brooklyn, NY. She is a highly sought after Brand Architect with an oasis of knowledge in various industries including Music, Fashion, Wine and Spirits, Television and most recently the Bottled water industry. Pittman is a powerful and respected force in the world of Marketing. Over the course of two decades, she held titles at media companies such as Time, Inc., Vibe Media Group and Conde Nast, before transitioning to the Blue Flame Agency where she sat as the VP of Marketing. Pittman's innovative approach, and strategic way of thinking lead to a Vice President position at Combs Enterprises, where she worked alongside executive teams, overseeing business objectives and long lead strategy. It was this position that catapulted her into a C – Suite position as Chief Marketing Officer of AQUAhydrate Inc.

After 20+ fulfilling years in the corporate sector, Pittman launched Epitome Media Group, a consulting company specializing in brand building with a primary focus on lifestyle, branding, and positioning. Her campaigns and initiatives have reached across genres, creating a bridge between influencers, artists, celebrities, brands and most importantly consumers. Having navigated a path to success amidst adversity; it is important to her to give back and to remain true to self. When she's not working, you can find Pittman mentoring youth, volunteering with her favorite nonprofits, traveling and creating new adventures somewhere quoting both Jay Z and Coco Chanel with ease.

Printed in Great Britain
by Amazon